Other Books by F.P. Nieman
Under Every Stone

THE SUNBAKED TIN CAN

F.P. NIEMAN

Copyright © 2014 Authored By F.P. Nieman
All rights reserved.

ISBN: 1500132551
ISBN 13: 9781500132552
Library of Congress Control Number: 2014910863
CreateSpace Independent Publishing Platform
North Charleston, South Carolina

Dedication

This book is dedicated to my brother Willie, whose intense love of life had enveloped and saturated me before I was even old enough to walk.

William Mark Nieman
April 25, 1956 – July 2, 2008

Acknowledgements

Thank you to my family and my friends, especially my son Zach, who proved to me that, "You can do it!" Thank you to my wife Linnea for your eternal patience and love. Thank you to my editor Liz, and to Jennifer, Janice, and Sarah for all your help and support. Thank you to my students. Your youthful enthusiasm has been a big source of positive energy in my life for over thirty years.

Table of Contents

Chapter 1	Brotherhood and the Mouse	1
Chapter 2	The Road	8
Chapter 3	Violins	14
Chapter 4	The 707	20
Chapter 5	The School and Blanca	26
Chapter 6	The General	30
Chapter 7	The Scalper	37
Chapter 8	The Train	42
Chapter 9	Cold Milk	54
Chapter 10	The Roof	58
Chapter 11	The Thump	66
Chapter 12	The Shack	74
Chapter 13	The Chicken	82
Chapter 14	The Font	94
Chapter 15	The Crane	99
Chapter 16	"My Town"	103
Chapter 17	The New Law	117
Chapter 18	The Strike	124

TABLE OF CONTENTS

Chapter 19	The Frog	133
Chapter 20	The Log	139
Chapter 21	The Pub	143
Chapter 22	The DC-3	152
Chapter 23	The Fever	160
Chapter 24	The Omelet	165
Chapter 25	La Paz	168

Foreword

I wrote this tale to pay tribute to the creativity, spontaneity, and resilience of youth. It is my hope that this true story will inspire all of us to remember and acknowledge the magic of innocence, the wonder of discovery, and the bold tenacity of inexperience in the face of challenge. This story is my attempt to capture and celebrate the boundless energy and indomitable spirit of the young as they explore the unknown, fail and rebound, and learn through trial and error to transform healthy naivety into wisdom.

CHAPTER 1

BROTHERHOOD AND THE MOUSE

"I look to the diffusion of light and education as the resource most to be relied upon for ameliorating the condition, promoting the virtue, and advancing the happiness of man."
—THOMAS JEFFERSON

When my parents brought me home from the hospital as a new baby, my brother Willie apparently took the words, "This is your new brother," literally. He was only one year and three days old when I was born, but he immediately took a deep personal interest in my well-being and in the development of my sense of adventure and love of freedom. He repeatedly

BROTHERHOOD

climbed into my crib and demonstrated the step-by-step procedure for escaping from the little jail cell, even before I could crawl. He took his afternoon nap on the floor next to my crib, sleeping on a makeshift bed of blankets he had gathered from around the house, and was generally delighted by my existence in every way. And once I learned how to escape from the crib, we were a team on a mission to explore the world.

As we grew up, our parents adorned the walls of our shared bedroom with pictures and posters. Some of them were photos, others were paintings or drawings. I was most attracted to the prints that featured confusing shapes and depicted random objects and distorted creatures. Unbeknownst to me, these convoluted sketches were maps, but to my young, untrained eye they stirred up much more in my imagination than the cartographer perhaps intended. One day, on one of the prints, a being took shape right before my eyes and emblazoned itself onto my memory. From then on, I could never look at that wall-hanging without having the peculiar beast pop into view and look back at me.

The creature both intrigued and disgusted me. Its nose was weak and fragmented and although I was

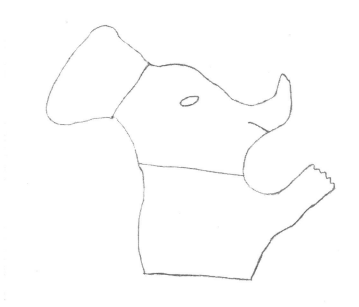

FIGMENT OF A YOUTHFUL IMAGINATION

only five years old, I knew that a proper nose needed to be more substantial—better defined, and not turned up. The eye was odd too. Overall, the thing looked like a conceited, deformed mouse. The hat was the best part of the hideous creature. It fit properly, was well shaped, and looked like a chef's hat. The disfigured hand and thick arm were useless, as was the only visible leg, and I stared at it often and wondered how this pathetic mouse could walk or do anything with its hands. Its mouth was also very small, especially for something with such a huge, awful head. There were oddities lurking in other places on the sketch too, but none was as overtly grotesque. Willie insisted I was making up nonsense. He said he couldn't see the mouse, but I showed it to him again and again and soon figured out that he actually did see it and was just pretending not to so he could continue to act like I was crazy. Since I was a year younger than Willie—and since older brothers think they know everything—he wanted me to capitulate and admit that there was no mouse, but I would not.

As the next few years passed, I gradually came to understand that the colorful drawing was a world map, but the relationship between my imaginary mouse and the places it represented on earth remained nebulous to me. Eventually, I recognized that the mouse's eye was the Canadian Great Bear Lake, the hat was Alaska, and the heavy, clubbed arm was Quebec. The head was Canada, and the main body was the United States. The leg was Mexico, and the puny little mouth was the Chesterfield Inlet to Baker Lake in the northeastern Canadian Territory of Nunavut. Even though I eventually outgrew my immature imaginings, I could never forget the mouse nor blithely pretend I had not been enchanted by something powerful. It had given me a personal connection, almost a familiarity with many distant places in the world. Moreover, there was a beckoning. Every glance at the map jarred me with a nagging sense of promise to one day visit the mouse's features. And though he would not admit it, the map had seduced Willie too.

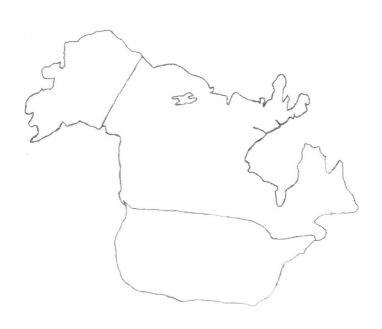

PART OF NORTH AMERICA

CHAPTER 2

THE ROAD

By our mid-teens, the mouse had become a faded childhood memory, but seeing the world continued to entice both of us. Our family of ten—which by then included eight children—moved often, so Willie and I had been introduced to travel by surviving half a dozen car trips across the United States. We had spent days on end covering thousands of miles in a 1963 Volkswagen bus, often with limited access to food, water, or a restroom. Incredibly, we developed an enjoyment of low-budget adventuring and refined it to an art. As soon as we each had a driver's license, we went out on the road by ourselves in old beat-up cars to explore different states. We plodded forth in heat or cold and became skilled at drafting big rigs and coasting down hills to use less gasoline. Most nights we ended up camping on the ground in sleeping bags, ideally for free in a parking lot or a farmer's field. This strategy never failed to get us through the necessary climate and landscape changes en route to our destinations. By age twenty-one, either by hitchhiking, car, bus, motorcycle, train, or plane, I had covered quite a bit of the United States, Europe, Canada, and Mexico. But I had not yet traveled to South America where Willie, by that time, had already spent nearly two years.

Willie was forever extolling the virtues of Latin America and urging me to venture farther south. I was wary of his enthusiasm, which usually radiated from him at a fever pitch. It was genuine for him but hollow in substance for my tastes. In our late teens, each of us had pursued his own destinations on his own terms, investigating whatever part of the world that had beckoned. We each had stood face to face with what had drawn us there, satiated ourselves, and then, bankrupt, weary and worn, returned home. We would reunite, usually in California. There, we told our tales, recharged our batteries, earned some more money, and then felt the lure set in again. Before long, we were planning the next trip and starting the process all over again.

When Willie reminisced about his travels, his memories were of the smells of different women, of vistas and heart-stopping dangers from the tops of gurgling volcanoes, of beautiful beaches, of free-flowing alcoholic beverages, and of places that couldn't easily be found on a map. He generally was satisfied to acquire just enough of the local idiom to get by. My memories included adrenaline-filled thrills as well, but also were interlaced with verb conjugations, grammar rules, and memorized nouns and pronouns. I wasn't willing to go anywhere unless the trip included a serious attempt to learn a new language.

In December of 1979, I was twenty-two years old and South America was next on my list. Willie muttered something about me finally coming to my senses and promptly announced that he would join me. I knew that his travel priorities were very different from mine, so I protested. But Willie assured me that he knew of a language school where we could both study Spanish. He reluctantly admitted that in the past his language-learning efforts had been less than stellar, but said he was finally ready to invest in mastering Spanish.

The school Willie had in mind was in Cochabamba, Bolivia. It was run by the Maryknoll priests and was supposedly one of the best of its kind. He suggested that we fly to Santa Cruz, Bolivia, make our way 8,000 feet up into the Andean foothills to the town of Cochabamba, find the school, sign up, and start learning. That was just what I wanted. Although Willie raved about the school, he had never actually attended it. He had tried, registering by mail from Columbia several years prior, but a bus ride from hell had delivered him two weeks late for a four-week course. As a result, he had been turned away with a partial refund. Nevertheless, he swore this was an excellent school, so we set out to go there.

We decided to coordinate our trip with an eccentric Swiss-German baker named Pablo, whom Willie had met several years earlier in Guatemala. Pablo had shown up in California looking for a job and a place to stay, which Willie had provided. Pablo had saved some money and was anxious to return to South America. He planned to leave a bit before we did, so Willie and I agreed to meet him in the main plaza of Santa Cruz at a date we would send to him by mail when we knew more precisely the details of our departure. Pablo left in early January and within two weeks, we followed.

SOUTH AMERICA

CHAPTER 3

VIOLINS

Leaving ourselves open to whatever might come, we bought one-way tickets to Santa Cruz with LAB, the Bolivian national airline. A day and a half and several stopovers later, we finally were almost there. As the plane tilted to the left, giving me a clear view of the city and taunting a fear of heights I was carefully holding in check, I mentioned to Willie that it seemed we were coming in over the slums. He leaned over me, looked for himself, and glanced at me like I couldn't possibly have seen the same thing he had just seen.

"Uh, no, that's not the slums," he said. "That's *it*." As I had countless times before in life, I dismissed him as delusional, and we glided in to touchdown.

The customs check area was very crowded and in a state of utter confusion. There was an extraordinarily heavy military presence, and most of the soldiers looked like fifteen-year-old kids. Their uniforms, helmets, holstered pistols, and loaded rifles—fingers on the triggers—didn't match up in the slightest with their boyish faces. Nevertheless, I knew enough to trust that what I saw was real. There was no clear system for getting through customs in an orderly manner. It was a chaotic mob scene in really slow motion. The stifling heat and humidity further drained our energy, adding to the misery and fatigue from the long flights. And it was nerve-racking to be surrounded by so many children with real machine guns.

Since waiting in line didn't seem to be a concept in Bolivia, Willie resurrected what he could remember about the fine art of working one's way forward through a crowd. The trick was to make progress without offending anyone, but there was no possible way to move forward without shoving, elbowing, squeezing, and taking advantage of even the slightest opportunity to get ahead. Too much courtesy and patience could easily result in a loss of ground. We watched with great frustration as several individuals, who had arrived long after we had, worked their way to the front, took care of business, and were soon on their way out of the airport. Nearly an hour passed and we were still wallowing in the sweltering nervousness and vivid olfactory experience of the middle of the crowd. Obviously, Willie was out of practice. Finally, we agreed that despite our efforts we were drifting farther and farther from the custom agent's desk, and Willie decided he had had enough. He solved our problem by increasing the pushing, shoving, and nudging just enough to clear people out of the way. His effort lacked the subtlety and finesse of the local experts, but it worked for a while. I stayed hot on his heels, and both of us tuned out the protestations of others as we made good progress. Soon the anger of the crowd reached a palpable critical mass of sorts, at which point Willie's instincts told him to stop pushing, but by then we were almost at the front.

Everyone in the entire customs check area was struggling toward one lone official on the other side of a long counter. The countertop to his right and left was covered with hundreds of copies of a small form. The forms were to be filled out and handed back to the customs agent along with the passport. After over an hour in the perspiration-soaked sea of humanity, we finally made it to the front. We each acquired one of the small papers, filled it out, handed it over, and after a sweeping and very dramatic signature by the officer, we were processed without incident. On our way out of the room, the view we had of the area behind the gentleman doing the paperwork revealed a pile of the little forms we had filled out. Although he made his job appear quite important and official, the man was actually "filing" the forms by throwing them over his shoulder onto the floor. Whenever a small gust of wind would wisp through the area, it would scatter the scraps all over the ground and even carry some of them out from behind the imposing counter. Looking down, we noticed we were trampling on quite a few as we exited. This led me to ponder whether there is an inverse relationship between a society's use of file cabinets and its need for firearms.

When we finally arrived in town, I didn't want to seem wimpy to Willie so I acted a lot less bothered by the heat and humidity than was actually the case. My attempt to appear unperturbed was further complicated by my desire not to stand out as a tourist. I took in as much as I could right from the start and was pleasantly impressed by how many violin players Bolivia apparently had. As we strolled along the sidewalks of Santa Cruz toward the part of town where we could find the cheapest hotel, I noticed one, then another, and then yet another violin-case store. I had never known a culture to have so many violins.

Oddly, I had seen no one playing the instrument, nor had I seen any violins for sale in the stores. But the abundance of the simple little cases made me certain there would be evidence of the instruments themselves at any minute. My curiosity got the better of me, so when we passed by yet another violin-case shop I asked Willie where all the violins were. He ignored me. I asked again. He ignored me again. As we walked past at least the fifth such store, I loudly reiterated my query.

"What the hell are you talking about?" he burst out. I shyly pointed to the store window and asked again. He snapped back impatiently: "Violins! What violins? You're an idiot. Those aren't violin cases. They're baby coffins!" I felt sort of sick and decided not to ask any more happy-go-lucky questions.

Even though the flights from San Francisco to Miami, to Panama, to Manaus, and then to Santa Cruz had gone well, I hadn't slept in over thirty-six hours and felt completely time-warped. I was so tired and numb I could barely figure out whether I was hungry or thirsty. We trudged through the downtown, followed our guidebook's directions to a cheap hotel very near the main plaza, and paid for a couple of days. The dingy room smelled like a dark closet no one had been in for years. It had two cots, a light bulb hanging from the ceiling by two wires, and a small table between the beds. Not bad for a dollar-fifty a night for the two of us.

We put most of our luggage in the room and then decided to head out to try to find Pablo and a place to eat. Back out in the bright afternoon, we located the main plaza and, finding no Pablo, we sat down at a table in a dimly lit restaurant and ordered a meal. After stuffing my empty stomach, an overwhelming fatigue enveloped me, and I insisted on going back to the hotel for a quick snooze. Willie wasn't tired, so he ventured out again in search of Pablo. Within thirty minutes, the door burst open and the two of them charged into the room laughing and talking.

CHAPTER 4

THE 707

Pablo wanted nothing to do with our language school, so we hung out with him for two days just for old times' sake and then decided to fly to Cochabamba, several hundred miles to the west. We found a travel agency where we could get tickets for twenty-nine dollars each. Everything was going quite smoothly until the young lady behind the counter needed to know how to spell our names. For some reason, pronouncing clearly didn't seem to help her at all, so Willie and I decided to avoid any further confusion by simply spelling our names for her. I didn't know the Spanish alphabet yet, but Willie did and he struggled mightily to help the clerk type our names into the computer. She pecked diligently at the keyboard, occasionally turning the screen our way so we could see if she had gotten it right, but the poor girl was utterly incapable of converting into print the carefully enunciated spelling of our first names. In a last-ditch effort, we tried saying our names in their Spanish translations. She smiled triumphantly and beamed as she typed. Then she needed the last name. Try as all three of us might, she was unable to get the first half of the word and ended up with only the last three letters of our family name, M-A-N. So there we were, Francisco and Guillermo Man. Memories of the rifle-toting teenagers fresh in my head, I fretted aloud to Willie that we could end up in trouble if the names on our tickets did not match the names in our passports. But he assured me that I need not worry.

We took our seats in the Boeing 707 and I noticed that the plane was nearly full. The quiet conversations of the passengers and the distant hum of the engines was abruptly shattered by a loud but friendly verbal outburst from the pilot as he walked down the main aisle of the aircraft and suddenly recognized an old pal. The two shook hands, hugged, laughed, slapped each other on the back, and talked excitedly. The pilot invited his friend to join him up in the cockpit, and the two disappeared. Shortly thereafter, a stewardess dutifully counted each passenger and, convinced that she had counted wrong, painstakingly counted again. It seemed that someone was missing. The stewardesses checked the bathrooms, mumbled into their walkie-talkies, huddled and strategized, and then did a recount. I knew my number. I was *diez y ocho*, or "eighteen," and I tried to say so when it was my turn to be counted, but the stewardess was not appreciative. After seven or eight recounts, exasperation set in. I suggested to Willie that they needed to be informed that the missing passenger was up front with the pilot, but Willie was sure they already knew that. Finally, in order to explain the delay to the captain, a stewardess went into the cockpit and was startled to find an extra person on the flight crew, the missing passenger. The pilot said his friend would be allowed to stay up front, and the problem was solved. I coughed out a frustrated *diez y nueve*, "nineteen," as the stewardess walked by, but she pretended not to notice, and we were off.

We soon reached cruising altitude. Blue skies afforded a good view of the landscape below, and I was looking forward to quenching my thirst with a freshly served cold drink. With no warning, the cola in my plastic cup miraculously lifted itself out and hung in space. My eyes caught the feat a fraction of a second before my stomach registered the thrill of zero gravity. The air filled with gasps and hoots—and everyone's drinks. I had hit "air pockets" before, but this one was worse than any I had ever experienced. Suddenly my airborne cola went sideways and into a fascinating corkscrew motion. In seconds, we were perpendicular to the ground and everything was still floating. With the force of a light fall, there was a startling return of gravity, but it didn't make sense because as I looked to my left out the window, I saw only the ground, and no horizon. The left wing was aiming straight down and the right one straight up, yet a powerful force pressed us into our seats rather than down to earth. Curiosity and excitement instantly turned to abject fear as passengers, freshly doused in soda, beer, and orange juice, realized we were completely sideways. A couple of rows in front of us, the stewardess lost an entire tray of drinks. First it floated upward and seemed to hang in the air, and then it spiraled sideways, splashing all over some unsuspecting people. In an instant, gravity again gained the upper hand, and the sideways plane's right-side overhead compartments swung open, dumping their contents onto the passengers seated on the left side of the plane. People started screeching, crying, praying, and panicking, but to no avail. Smoothly and without so much as a bump, the barrel roll continued. In a few more seconds we were perfectly upside down, and then we continued around until the plane was again sideways but on the opposite side from before. Soon it was the right-side passengers' turn to receive the obligatory overhead-contents pummeling. Then, predictably, the counterclockwise whirl finally brought the plane back around to where the roll had started. As quickly as it had struck, the amusement-park ride was over. The captain dropped the plane into a high-speed, swooping descent, made a perfect landing, decelerated on the tarmac with unusually high G-force, and then gently rolled into our gate at a walking pace. Passengers were in tears, some dripping with beverages, others bruised and battered by falling luggage. Worse yet, quite a few had tumbled through the entire 360-degree roll with their seat belts unfastened. Aghast but unhurt, I felt the plane stop and heard a distant enthusiasm over the wailing of the upset passengers. The cajoling, hooting, and cackling became even more intense as the pilot and his buddy exited the cockpit. They talked and laughed nonstop as they walked off the plane, oblivious to anything but the screaming success of their little daredevil prank.

CHAPTER 5

THE SCHOOL AND BLANCA

The air in Cochabamba was considerably thinner, cooler, and less humid than it had been in the Santa Cruz lowlands. The soda and beer on our clothes and in our hair was drying into a sticky mess, so Willie and I agreed to spend a little more money on lodging if it meant having running water and being able to bathe. We ended up near the main plaza on the third floor of a hotel with a very nice balcony. We strolled around to get our bearings and decided to try to find the language school on foot. Nearly an hour later, we were on the outskirts of town, more than a mile down a dirt road, and I was sure Willie was lost. He said he trusted his own internal compass implicitly and pointed out that I had absolutely no sense of direction. He suggested that I relax and assured me that we would find the school. He was right. I had not even the remotest idea where we were, and on his previous trip he had spent considerable time in that general area. So I trudged on and was abruptly startled by his announcement.

"There it is."

The Catholic facility that stood in the distance looked almost exactly as I had imagined it, and it lifted both of our spirits. This was, after all, the very reason we had traveled all this way. For me, probably more than for Willie, this place was like the prize at the end of a long, drawn-out treasure hunt. The school was quiet and monastery-like. We entered and soon found a delicate and soft-spoken receptionist. She agreed to fetch someone with more authority, as she was unable to answer all of our questions. The director, an American priest, walked into the room and immediately recognized Willie. They exchanged pleasantries and mutually lamented Willie's prior failed attempt at attending the school. We then got down to business and although he was as formal and polite as possible, the director dropped a bomb on our plan, demolishing in a few minutes what we had planned for months. A very popular magazine in the United States, it seemed, had sent a journalist to the school shortly after Willie's first attempt to enroll. The journalist had written such a glowing review that the school had subsequently been flooded by students and was fully booked up, with a waiting list for at least the next ten months. The news left us feeling very let down and empty. There were other language schools in Bolivia, of course, but attending this one had been our goal.

Willie was grumbling about this being his second failed attempt to learn Spanish at this same school when the director signaled us to huddle closer. First, he gave each of us one of the school's business cards and hand-wrote on the back that we were to be granted library privileges at the school any time it was open. He then rather secretively passed us a note with the name and address of one of the school's recently retired teachers, Blanca, who now gave private lessons and would surely teach us Spanish as well as the school would have. We thanked the director and, half-defeated, half-victorious, walked back down the dirt road into town and to Blanca's house. We knocked on her door and waited nervously. No answer. We knocked again and were just about to leave when we heard footsteps. The door opened slowly and before us stood four feet four inches of kindness, professionalism, and educated dignity.

"Let me guess," she started. "The school sent you."

We introduced ourselves, explained our situation, and she sighed and seemed to genuinely empathize.

"I, too, am booked up solid," she said. "But one student who now has two hours a day will be leaving in just over two weeks. If you want his 10:00 a.m.-to-noon time slot, you need to commit to it now."

We agreed and shook on it. Blanca wrote down our names, thanked us, and smiled warmly.

"See you in a couple of weeks," she said.

We then found a bar and celebrated. Killing some time was not a problem for Willie or me. We had our lessons all lined up, and the world was our oyster.

CHAPTER 6

THE GENERAL

Willie realized before I did that it was the time of year when people in Latin America celebrated various versions of *Carnaval*. The long-standing Bolivian tradition of throwing water at friends, family or even total strangers, was in full swing. Each year, only during these two weeks near the end of January, it was socially acceptable, even encouraged, to bombard anyone in sight with water. The assault might come from a bucket, a squirt gun, a hose, or a water balloon, all in good fun. In fact, Willie and I had been on the receiving end of several onslaughts between Blanca's house and the bar, usually from giggling teenage girls. We were quicker to react than they had anticipated and we had successfully dodged most of the water. After a couple of beers, the topic of all the public water-throwing came up, and we both foresaw that our years of playing baseball in parking lots was about to pay off. We decided to buy a large number of balloons, retreat to the balcony of our third-floor hotel room, scrounge up a tub for our ammunition, and launch a proper American water-balloon attack on the locals below.

Weak, gravity-powered water pressure from a storage tank on the roof above us slowed our pace a bit, but eventually, beer in one hand and water balloon in the other, we let loose. It seemed almost morally wrong the way we bombarded the first few victims. They didn't have a chance and didn't even know which way to run. For most of them, our precise air strike probably felt like being slapped sharply by an invisible enemy. Although we were convinced that what we were doing was completely socially appropriate, we were pushing the limits of fairness by the way the salvo came from above, silent and all but invisible. After a number of spectacular bull's-eyes, the targets below figured us out. In a matter of minutes, total strangers were alerting their fellow passersby, pointing up at us, ducking, running, and waving their arms to block the next volley.

A group of three young men in their early twenties decided to go get their own artillery and have a standoff with us then and there. They never had a chance. Their throws, thirty feet uphill and over a balcony wall were no match for the shots from our baseball-honed throwing arms. Furthermore, our launches were aided by gravity and the fact that we had cover, while they were out in the open. It was a slaughter. Soaked and out of ammunition in minutes, they openly admitted defeat and surrendered. They then had the good humor to ask if they could come into the hotel and join us on our balcony. We decided it wasn't a trap and even if it was, we figured we could take them, so we obliged.

A few minutes later, there they were, dripping wet, smiling, introducing themselves, and eager to try to do to someone below what we had just done to them. They wasted a lot of balloons before one finally found its target, and Willie and I concluded that Bolivians obviously did not play enough baseball or skip enough rocks at the beach. We also agreed that the camaraderie was worth much more than the misfired balloons.

THE SUNBAKED TIN CAN

Just as we were running low on ammo and it seemed we would have to pick our last remaining targets carefully and be done with the fun, Willie saw a large military truck moving slowly down the street with traffic. Most car drivers had the good sense to keep their windows rolled up, although it was still quite a score to slam a balloon perfectly onto a roof, hood, or windshield. Now, along came the large truck with the wing window open on the driver's side. Willie announced that the open window was his, but was met with loud, immediate protestations by our new friends. It seemed that the water free-for-all included everyone except members of the military. And the truck with the vulnerable, open window was not just any military vehicle, but apparently one driven by a very high-ranking officer. Willie was unfazed. As he wound up to hurl the balloon, the Bolivians panicked, ducked behind the balcony wall, and begged Willie to reconsider. They were convinced that this was a terrible mistake and worried out loud that there could be some very serious, negative consequences for nailing an unsuspecting colonel or general. Willie, visibly savoring the irreverence and unmitigated audacity of it all, let the balloon fly. It was a perfect shot. The undulating, high-speed orb sailed directly to the open, angled window, ricocheted into the cab of the truck and landed right in the driver's lap, exploding as it hit home. Our Bolivian buddies, imagining it had missed, dared to sneak a glance over the balcony wall only to see the truck skid to a halt at the same time Willie and I burst into laughter and exchanged high fives. They knew their worst fear had come true, and they were genuinely afraid. They were pleading with us to keep quiet and hide as the *generalissimo* leaped from the truck. He was red in the face with rage and he was flapping his arms accusingly as he stomped around and accosted everyone in sight. He was angry as all hell, and he looked for all the world like someone who had just urinated in his pants.

People were fleeing the area as if for their lives, and a rare mixture of comedy and tragedy played out as this immensely powerful man simultaneously ranted, threatened, and pouted in the middle of the street. He stopped traffic in both directions and frantically looked around for whoever had nailed him, his dignity fading with every passing second. And yet, as had been the case with our first few victims, it never occurred to him to look up.

By now, Willie and I had taken the hint that this was serious business and had gone into stealth mode. We were spying on the scene from behind the balcony wall, and I was actually beginning to fear what might happen to us if this guy caught us. Then, in one of the more defiant moves I may ever see in my life, when the general turned his back, Willie, without saying a word, grabbed a balloon and scored another perfect shot. It slammed the indignant *jefe* right in the middle of the upper back, and I could almost hear all of his medals jingle as he twitched from the impact. Soaked and humiliated beyond all repair, the general hustled back to his big truck, jumped in, revved it up as if in a drag race, and launched the truck down the road. The street in front of him was empty of cars, but pedestrians scurried for the sidewalks as he blasted forward, full-throttle, leaving behind an enormous cloud of diesel smoke and even a little burned rubber.

Willie and I were instantly heroes. There was a lot of commotion down on the street below, and the people there who had known all along who hit the general, but had not snitched on us, cheered us. Our buddies on the balcony, shaken but relieved as after a near-death experience, suggested we all head to a favorite nearby bar to celebrate.

CHAPTER 7

THE SCALPER

With a bit more than two weeks to kill before our classes started, we boarded a flight back to Santa Cruz. On the way, Willie had a great idea. He suggested we go to Rio de Janeiro for *Carnaval*, which was starting in a few days and would last about two weeks. Then we would zip back to Cochabamba just in time for our Spanish lessons. The only problem was that the train ride east from Santa Cruz to Brazil was reputed to be awful. So Willie calculated that we should fly the 550-mile distance from Santa Cruz to Corumbá on the Bolivian-Brazilian border, and then use the comfortable, modern Brazilian train system for the remaining 1,150 miles to Rio. Taking the train in Brazil, rather than flying, would save us lots of money and we could still be in Rio in time for all the fun. It seemed Willie had the whole adventure planned out, so I agreed to go along.

Back in Santa Cruz, we located Pablo and told him of the Rio plan. He loved the idea and jumped at the chance to join us. We packed our things, headed to the airport, and found the only ticket window that still had flights to Brazil. Judging by the size of the tightly packed crowd, we weren't the only ones who wanted to go to *Carnaval*. We waded into the sweltering throng and engaged in the usual nudge-press-squirm method of getting up to the counter. As we approached, we could make out that most of the people were buying tickets just to the border, thereby avoiding the train for the Bolivian leg of the journey. It was almost our turn when the man immediately in front of us began his transaction with the clerk. He cleared a generous space to his right and left with his elbows, hefted a briefcase up onto the counter and proceeded to buy, with cash, every single remaining ticket on every flight to the border town of Corumbá.

As if that wasn't bad enough, the airline employee, with no more tickets to sell, closed the window at the ticket counter, locked up, turned off the light, and left her station. We weren't sure exactly what was going on, but we patiently waited in the hope that, one way or another, we would leave with some airline tickets. Within minutes, the man with the briefcase had gone around behind the desk, flipped the light back on, and was selling the tickets he had just purchased for thirty dollars, for twice that amount. Some people were outraged and left, but others didn't flinch at the new, doubled price. Pablo, Willie, and I decided we would not line this guy's pockets at any price and angrily left the airport, agreeing to go by train.

There was the usual hustling and wheeling and dealing going on when we arrived at the humid but dusty train station. We bore into the small mob to try to get a ticket from Santa Cruz to Puerto Suarez, at the end of the rail line, on the Brazilian border. I thought I heard Pablo say something in Swiss German, but it didn't make sense because he was very close to me and the voice had come from somewhere else in the crowd. I heard it again and focused in the direction of the foreign language to see a group of four European-looking fellows in their early twenties, chatting loudly in Swiss German. The crowd yielded as we gently persuaded people to let us through, and in a matter of minutes, Willie, Pablo, and I were introducing ourselves to the Swiss guys. After a minute of chatting, we discovered that they intended to go to the border on the same train, and then on to Rio. They all had very different personalities but had been friends for quite some time. Peter was the tallest of the four and very talkative, and Klaus was high-energy, witty, light on his feet, and constantly cracking jokes. Then there was Hans, observant, more of a listener than a talker, and Steffen, logical, levelheaded, and at about age twenty-six, the oldest of the group.

Willie seemed mildly irritated since he was the only one who could not speak German, but his background in anthropology and years of travel had rendered him a consummate *Menschenkenner*—connoisseur of human nature—so he never missed anything important. We bought our tickets and agreed to kill a few hours and then meet back at the train at about five thirty that evening.

PERTINENT BOLIVIAN CITIES
AND THE TRAIN TRACKS

CHAPTER 8

THE TRAIN

I was not yet accustomed to the Bolivian concept of punctuality and thus suffered from the ridiculous delusion that the train would leave at the established 6:00 p.m. departure time. When we boarded the old, much-abused train car, most of the seats were empty. The wooden floors appeared to have been trampled upon by every imaginable sort of shoe, boot, paw, and hoof. Apparently, it also had endured heavy, wheeled carts, dragged pallets, and sordid cargo for half a century. Stains bore witness to every liquid that ever had been spilled, and there were jagged holes here and there through which one could see the ground and the tracks below. A few spots looked as though they had been on fire at one point or another. All of the windowpanes were gone, having been broken out many years earlier. From the ceiling hung a single row of fluorescent bulbs dangling from wires and fixtures that had been ripped loose eons ago. The musty old car smelled like an odd mix of farm animals, dilapidated machinery, and jungle. The train was not unusually long, with fifteen to twenty cars. Following the engine was a flat car with no sides and then seven or eight large, sealed boxcars with no windows. After that were seven or eight passenger cars and finally a traditional caboose.

Pablo, Willie, the Swiss guys, and I settled into one of the passenger cars and tried to relax for the long ride, which we had been told would take about twenty hours. Six o'clock rolled around, and I noticed that the train did not move an inch. Oddly, the people milling about on the platform were behaving as though they didn't expect it to leave any time soon. There was nothing to do but wait. Seven o'clock passed and then eight, and then nine. By ten o'clock it was dark outside, but still there was no departure. The delay particularly annoyed the Swiss Germans and me, as we all had experienced train travel in Switzerland and Germany, where punctuality is placed on a pedestal next to godliness. A lone French girl who appeared to be in her early twenties was seated across the aisle, several rows behind us. I tried to have a friendly chat with her but she would have none of it, preferring to keep to herself. For reasons I couldn't understand, she, Willie, and all of the Bolivian passengers seemed unfazed by the four-hour delay that irritated the Swiss guys and me to no end. We continued to sit and wait as, little by little, the train filled up with passengers, mostly locals.

Shortly after ten thirty, the train finally began to creak and clank as it slowly clattered out of the station and into the night. Within thirty minutes, we had left Santa Cruz far behind us and were surrounded by a sultry, sweet-smelling night, thick with jungle on both sides of the train. In the long row of fluorescent bulbs that ran the length of our car, only one actually worked—and it flickered nervously, lighting the interior very poorly at best. As I stared at the light bulb, I noticed a rather busy swarm of small flying bugs that I thought were gnats or mosquitos. I already had gotten fifteen or twenty mosquito bites in only the first half hour of the ride. It crossed my mind that I might have to fight the whole night through, slapping one mosquito after another, but I also imagined their numbers might diminish as we distanced ourselves from the city.

An hour into the trip, the train was chugging along at a slow, rhythmic pace of maybe twenty miles per hour and was emitting a regular, repetitious set of very unpleasant sounds. My ear, trained in auto mechanics, told me that everything on the train was screaming out for lubrication. It sounded to me like nothing had been greased since the thing was built. Suddenly, the grinding, groaning sounds changed pitch, and new screeching, creaking noises intermingled into a disgusting cacophony as the train began to slow down. We stopped within a hundred yards, but before we did, mosquitos swarmed the train car. I was now getting more new bites every minute than I had gotten during the whole first hour of the trip. There we were, stopped in the middle of a swampy jungle at the southern end of the great Amazon Delta, on a train sporting a flickering fluorescent light, with no screens or windows. The train was a huge bug light, a mosquito magnet, a baited flying-insect trap, but in this case it was the bait that would die instead of the bugs. The train was stopped, but in our group everything else started to move very quickly. Willie, the Swiss guys, and I jumped out of our seats within the first few seconds after stopping and began a frantic Saint Vitus dance—slapping, squirming, grabbing at the air, and doing anything we could to avoid the mosquitos and kill as many of them as possible. We took to aiding each other by randomly hitting any mosquito we saw on someone else. Soon we were all bouncing around the car, arms flailing as we smacked each other in a horrible, hysterical effort to avoid being overwhelmed by the hungry predators.

These mosquitos were unusually large compared to the ones I had encountered in other parts of the world. The little probes through which they sucked blood were much more heavy-duty than usual, so getting stabbed by one was a little like getting poked by a needle. The swarm was feasting on us to such an extent that within about five minutes, we started to notice that some of the mosquitos we swatted and killed would explode into a splatter of blood because they had just gorged themselves, hopefully on someone else. Soon our clothing and any exposed skin were covered in nickel- to quarter-sized bloodstains and the smeared corpses of mosquitos. The fierce, flying army was relentless. They dug into our hair and tried to go down our shirts or sleeves, up our pants legs, into our ears, up our noses, or into our mouths. There were thousands of them and they seemed to keep coming no matter how many we killed. Just when it seemed we would either lose the battle or need a drastically new plan, the train strained and grunted and started moving forward again. We had stopped for less than an hour, but we felt like we had spent every second of it in an active combat zone.

As the train slowly accelerated, we continued to fend off any new attacks and soon noticed a precipitous drop in the sheer number of mosquitos. Sure enough, as we picked up speed and killed the ones remaining on the train, we began to get ahead of the game. Apparently, at more than twenty miles an hour, it was much more difficult for them to come in through the various openings than when we were stopped. I also noticed that the native Bolivians seated all around us seemed immune to the assault. The mosquitos totally ignored them and only attacked the *gringos*. Our bodies and egos bitten and bruised, our gang of seven settled down, each with his own thoughts. We wondered aloud, angrily, why the train had stopped in the first place and why the light had been left on, rendering us so vulnerable. Our resentment and vitriol ebbed and flowed, and eventually we decided to lick our wounds and try to get some sleep.

Then the train stopped again. Just as before, the bugs swarmed in. Again we were stormed from all sides. Again we flailed about, striving mightily to fend off their blood-sucking bites. We could tell by looking at each other that areas of the body not constantly swatted would attract enormous numbers of mosquitos. It was possible to kill as many as a dozen of the pests with one well-placed swat, such as in the middle of another person's back. Most of the locals had left our car by this point, having quietly slipped out to find seats where there was less chaos and mayhem. The young French lady seemed to have things much better under control than we did, leading us to wonder if perhaps she had a secret stash of potent bug repellent that she didn't want to share. After another forty-five-minute episode of World War III, the train again started to move. As we continued, with ever-improving skill, to kill every flying thing in sight, the gross volume again declined to the point that we could actually sit down and try to relax. After the first attack, we had wiped off the messiest blood spatters and picked the chunks of dead mosquito off of our T-shirts and skin, and out of our hair, ears, and noses. But this time we didn't bother. We were experiencing a combination of exhaustion, triumph, and futility, and we began to choose more carefully where to put our energy. The blood-spatter problem had at first seemed merely gross and morbidly fascinating but was now beyond repair. Each one of us was covered with countless splotches of blood, our own as well as that of other people on the train. Some samples were quite large and wet, having not fully soaked into the shirt, and they smeared onto the seats and everything else they touched.

After the second assault, the mood in our train car changed somewhat. We now realized that being angry wasn't going to change anything. Bickering or even commiserating wasn't going to help either. Breaking the light would be a terrible idea because the mosquitos would surely find us anyway if the train stopped again, and without the light, we would not be able to see and kill them. Worse yet, we figured we were most likely going to continue to randomly stop and be terrorized, perhaps throughout the entire night. And that is exactly what happened. After three or four rounds of the same scenario, the nightmare became routine. Between salvos, I sat huddled on my seat and tried to count the hours and even the minutes we had remaining, trapped on the horrible train. I tried to convince myself that, because we had been told the trip would last twenty hours, we would arrive in Puerto Suarez at two o'clock the following afternoon. I struggled to reassure myself that the train officials had known about, and taken into account, the four-hour delay of our departure. Surely, I told myself, when they said the trip would take twenty hours, they had included the many stops in the night. Clearly, they could not expect paying customers to get out a stopwatch and stop the clock every time the train ceased to make progress. Undoubtedly, they were familiar with the train's route and routine. Surely, they all had, at one point or another, ridden this same train to Puerto Suarez. Yes, when they had said twenty hours, they had said so knowing full well what they were talking about. Or so I fantasized as I tried to fall asleep.

By dawn, we were a pathetic, very unhappy little group. The train sputtered and rattled slowly onward, frequently stopping for long periods of time for no apparent reason. When it stopped, the combination of heat, humidity, and stagnant air inside the train produced a truly miserable environment. But at least during the daylight hours we were not being bitten by anything. In fact, the air seemed remarkably insect-free. The late morning was gradually becoming midday, and I began to feel reenergized in my belief that the ordeal would soon be over. I checked my watch nervously and frequently, and did some quick math each time to see how much longer I would have to sit and wallow in other people's blood and my own perspiration. Occasionally I got a whiff of something rather putrid. I convinced myself that it had been there unnoticed all along, but it seemed to intensify with every passing hour. I wiped my forehead with the short sleeve of my T-shirt and realized the smell was coming from the hundreds of dead bugs and dried crust that covered me. A close inspection revealed that we had been doing battle with all sorts of odd creatures, not just mosquitos.

Rather than waste energy by becoming upset, I put into practice a defense mechanism I had learned long before. I withdrew inside my mind to a place that is almost removed from my body. In that mental state, my inner tranquility was almost impenetrable, protected from external storms. I had always been able to find safety there when the world became intolerable. I didn't use this strategy often because I was afraid I would wear out its extraordinary powers to numb physical pain, fade noise, and provide muted distance between my spirit and my body. This situation, however, called for extra-strong medicine.

Soon I dreaded looking at my watch. I couldn't face the fact that the magical time—2:00 p.m.—would come and go and we would not be at our destination. I braced myself for the worst and, of course, two o'clock came and went without anyone but me looking out the windows to see if we were coming into a town. The hours passed slowly. By ten thirty, night had descended upon us again and we endured another series of horrific battles with all sorts of flying, biting creatures. By sunrise, all of us were physically and mentally spent, and it was no small matter that by this point we were out of food and drinking water. We had been told the trip would take twenty hours and had duly prepared ourselves with provisions for that time frame. We had entrusted the train officials with our health and safety, and to deliver us on time, and they had not held up their end of the bargain.

CHAPTER 9

COLD MILK

It was late morning and the ambient temperature was steadily rising. In our group, we were mostly keeping to ourselves and perspiring incessantly as we slowly trundled forth in our squeaky, sunbaked tin can on wheels. The numerous Bolivians who had sought a more peaceful train car the night before had returned and had quietly settled back in. Klaus was sitting next to me on the right side of the train, near the window. He elbowed me and leaned in a little.

"Do you know what I want?" he asked in a dry, scratchy voice. He sounded calm but his tone was unusually serious and determined. It struck me as odd that he had spoken in English rather than in German. I leaned toward him and good-naturedly mocked his heavy German accent.

"No, I don't know *vaht* you *vahnt*," I said.

"Well," he answered, "I want a glass of cold milk." His accent made it sound like, "*Vell, I vahnt a glaahs of kohlt milch.*"

I said that was a great idea and that I, too, wanted a glass of cold milk. He sighed and leaned back away from me into his normal sitting position. He sat there very quietly for about thirty seconds and then, with no warning, bolted to his feet.

"*I vahnt a glaahs of kohlt milch!*" he shouted at the top of his lungs.

I started to stand up and tell him to calm down but then I saw his face. He looked crazed. He shoved his way past me and climbed over the backpacks and clutter on his way to the main corridor. He appeared oblivious to his surroundings and continued to scream over and over, "*I vahnt a glaahs of kohlt milch!*" In seconds he had the undivided attention of everyone in our train car. He wheeled around, glaring up and down the central corridor as if to decide which direction to go in, and began a rampage of accosting everyone, one bench seat at a time. He hollered in people's faces as loudly as he could at very close range that he "*vahnted a glaahs of kohlt milch.*" His rant continued to intensify and soon he was grabbing total strangers by the shoulders and briefly shaking them as he yelled. Within a few minutes, he had stomped his way from one end of the car to the other and made his desire for milk extremely clear to everyone.

I felt especially sorry for the otherwise calm and dignified Bolivian natives, who never seemed to complain despite the horrendous conditions. When Klaus first launched into his tirade, however, I saw abject fear in their faces. As he stormed hither and thither, assaulting everyone in his path with his insane demands for milk, people behind him were frantically gathering up their children and their belongings, and were pushing and stumbling over each other as they tried to escape through the doors at each end of the car. By the time the outburst was over, our car was nearly empty and a small crowd had gathered at both ends to watch the spectacle from a safe distance. As curiosity about the ruckus built, the word spread that another gringo had gone *loco*. And then as quickly as he had lost it, cold-milk boy regained his composure. Klaus returned to his seat next to me and sat quietly as if nothing remotely out of the ordinary had taken place. I made a mental note to buy him a liter of cold milk at the nearest opportunity.

CHAPTER 10

THE ROOF

As everyone settled back down and tried to relax in the jostling rhythm of the ride, some of the people who had fled in terror cautiously returned to their seats. For most of the ride I had been so focused on external threats that I had tuned out just how hungry, tired, and dehydrated I was. It was shortly after noon and already over a hundred degrees in our car. I did a quick time check: We had been on the train for forty-two hours and we were twenty-two hours overdue. We had long since run out of food and water, and we were in desperate need of bathing and clean clothing. The smell in the car was no longer merely an occasional whiff of something that had died, but was a constant, pungent reminder of the casualties suffered in the nightly battles with all things flying.

As suddenly as Klaus had decided that he wanted cold milk, Willie sprang to his feet and walked pointedly in my direction. He stopped and looked me directly in the face.

"I have had enough of this heat and this stench and I'm going up on the roof for some fresh air," he announced impatiently.

"Yeah, that would be nice. Too bad we can't do that," I said to him. My attempt to downplay his plan only fueled his determination to go through with it.

"Oh yes we can," he snapped back. "I'm going up there. You can do anything you want in Bolivia. It's kind of like the Wild West. But if you fall off the roof, they won't stop for you. I'm tired of this heat, and I'm outta here." With that, he turned away from me and headed down the aisle as if he were on a mission.

I fairly leaped out of my seat to follow him. Klaus understood some of what we had said and started to mutter at me as if to ask what had just transpired, but I took off and ignored him. Willie walked through several cars, pausing in the loud and jerky sections between them to get a good look at the hardware. Sure enough, he quickly located a small ladder that led up to the roof. It was solidly fixed in place. The ladder was quite narrow and offered poor lateral support, especially given the incessant swaying of the train, but it was adequate. I watched as Willie calculatedly pulled his large frame up against the primitive structure and awkwardly began the 90-degree vertical ascent. Within seconds he had vanished and was presumably on the roof. I followed and was just getting the hang of the distance between the rungs when I heard a commotion below me and glanced down to see five enthusiastic Swiss faces looking up and cheering me on. I rounded the corner and was on the roof. It was very hot, very dirty, and almost flat. I looked toward the rear of the train to see Willie well advanced and scooting away from me on his stomach.

Two long parallel rows of wooden beams, like two-by-fours, ran the length of each of the cars down the middle. They were about two feet apart and an inch or two off the roof, and were mounted every four feet or so with a bracket. I imagined they were there so cargo could be put on the roof and secured with rope, but I saw no such cargo. Willie had worked his way from the side of the car, where the ladder had been, to the center so he could take advantage of the luggage rails. I crawled soldier-style to the center and felt a lot better when I had something to grab onto. My blood-stained, dead-bug-ridden T-shirt and blue jeans were mopping up the dirt and filth from decades of the train's jungle excursions, yet I resolutely did not care. A new energy and verve swept through me. I felt like things were looking up—and I was secretly delighted at having possibly committed an act of civil disobedience against the Bolivian train company and even the train itself. They both deserved it for what they had put me through.

I could hear laughter and expressions of sheer delight as, one by one, the Swiss guys all scurried onto the roof. Willie had made it to the end of the car and had stopped and turned around to watch us slither and crawl toward him. Soon we were all together in a small cluster, giving each other high-fives and smiling uncontrollably as we rejoiced in our newfound freedom and sense of empowerment. We finally had found a way to let out days of pent up misery and anger. It felt cooler too, and the fresh breeze gave us a break from the stagnant humidity and foul odor below. There were other problems on the roof, such as the relentless, searing sun, but the tradeoff was welcome. In time, sunburn would drive us back down into the shaded oven below us, but for the moment the fresh air and that just-unleashed feeling dogs know so well was ours—and it was pure bliss.

Willie was the first to dare to try to stand up. His admonition—that if we fell, we would be abandoned in the jungle to die—was fresh in my mind, so I tensed up as I watched him try to stand and sway in counterbalanced sync with the side-to-side motion of the train. His knees were bent, ready to fold and drop him to the surface at any second as he pushed to stay longer and longer in a semi-upright position. As foot placement and traction became familiar to him, Willie slowly stood up. He was a natural. Within a minute he was almost fully upright, looking a lot like a surfer on the biggest surfboard ever made. Then came his first steps. Sure enough, he was able to compensate for the roof's movement and walk. It wasn't long until the rest of us were at it too. In very short order, we were running up and down the train car with ease.

True to his daring character, Willie was soon wondering aloud whether he could run and leap from one car to the other. We all agreed that the distance was not excessive and that the hardest part would be to match the landing with the predicted movement of the other car's roof. Each train car was actually swaying to its own beat, no single car matching the motion of any other. On any given car, it was easy to learn the rhythm, as was watching an adjacent car and learning its pattern as well. Coordinating a launch from one to another was a different story, however. In typical fashion, away Willie went with no warning, planting a perfect touchdown and getting seamlessly into the flow of the new car. The rest of us were not as athletic as he was, but in a short while we all were running up and down the length of the entire train, jumping from one car to the next with barely any hesitation. Up near the front, the noise was deafening and the air quality was horrible as the engine pumped out huge amounts of choking, black smoke. The farther toward the rear we went, the better the air quality got, and the noise level decreased so we could talk without having to yell.

THE ROOF

The cars felt like they swayed much more on the roof than down below, inside. Looking forward over the length of the pathetic contraption, I was surprised to see just how much chaos there was in the train's sway and just how random the movement of one car was relative to that of the others. Some were rather steady, and others leaned so far they looked like they were on the verge of tipping over. The car mechanic in me insisted that I climb down and take a good look at the suspension, especially on the cars with the most severe sway. I found so many loose, squeaking, dry parts that I was amazed the thing was still rolling and able to hold itself up. As I climbed back onto the roof, I was somewhat concerned but also resigned to the extreme limitations of what I could do about it.

The view from up top was otherworldly. Ahead, the tracks glistened as straight as an arrow into the distance, seemingly off into infinity. Directly behind lay the same scene, indistinguishable except for the visual effect caused by the different angle of the sun. To the right and left of the tracks was a clearing of perhaps fifty feet, and beyond that was one of the most awesome sights I had ever seen—endless, impenetrable, virgin jungle. It looked like something right out of a picture book. I found it sobering that for hundreds of miles in every direction there was nothing except more of the same pristine land, essentially unchanged from when dinosaurs roamed the earth. I felt privileged to be able to see a piece of the world exactly as it would have been if man had never set foot on this planet. I felt small against its vastness, no greater than one of the many mosquitos in the huge jungle's midst.

CHAPTER 11

THE THUMP

We had run to the front and then to the back of the train, leaping the gap between cars with aplomb for the better part of half an hour. The routine got old after a while, however, just as repeatedly riding the same roller coaster diminishes the excitement in relation to the initial thrill. We eventually sat down to relax on the roof of the ninth or tenth car. We sat in a row down the center, one behind the other, holding onto the luggage rack and facing forward. I was in the front and could hear muffled talking behind me. I had concluded that I shouldn't stay on the roof much longer because, fresh breeze or not, we were all becoming incredibly sunburned and dehydrated. I could see it in the red, shiny faces of the others and feel it on my own face and arms. But for the moment I was relaxed, looking on the bright side of things, and enjoying what I could of the remaining few minutes on the roof. I was watching the mesmerizing motion of the long row of train cars in front of me when one of them appeared to jump a few inches and then lean much too far. I suddenly felt a distinct thump. I tensed up as I tried to see what was happening and then felt a sharp jolt.

I couldn't understand what was going on. How could the third or fourth car of a train run over something that the first few cars had missed? Then the reality set in. The car that had hopped a bit had leaned too far to the right and had slipped off the tracks, causing the thumping sensation. Instead of righting itself after leaning and slipping, it had simply continued the slow descent over onto its side, pulling the car behind it down too. The car behind that one, in an extreme lean to the left, also began to fall, having been yanked off the tracks by the two unstable cars in front of it. The train was derailing.

Everything seemed to go into slow motion. Then, in an instant, the noise level rose exponentially. The train cars were systematically falling over, either to the right or the left, one by one, just like dominos. The screeching, clanking sounds were terrifying and so was the amount of dust and flying debris. It was like a bomb had gone off. The power of the engine had ceased to pull us forward, but our inertia was carrying us into a grinding mass of pure chaos. I could feel us decelerating, but the cars ahead of us continued to fall over, in order, at almost even intervals. It was only a matter of time until it would be our turn. I had mere seconds to make a plan. I noted that as the cars tipped over onto their sides, some would slide, and others would dig into the earth, plowing massive ditches as their momentum carried them. Yet others would flip over or rotate violently, crushing or clearing away everything in their path.

The only predictable part of the whole event was the surreal, seemingly slow-motion tipping over, as each car delicately leaned ever farther until it clashed in battle with the passing ground. The sheer brutality of the unfolding scene was most intimidating, and a part of me acknowledged that these might be the last few seconds of my life. Like a cornered animal, I relied on instinct for what to do. In a flash, I grasped the rails of the luggage rack with my hands and tucked my feet up under myself like a frog. From that position, I would be able to spring as far as possible on demand. I decided that, as the car tipped over, I would hold on as long as I could, no matter the angle, until the moment just before the side of the car hit the ground and all hell broke loose. Then at precisely the right instant, I would spring to the side, as if from an ejection seat, and tumble and roll as far as possible away from the impact zone. My greatest hope was that the car wouldn't spin out or flip over and land on top of me. I honestly gave no thought to the guys behind me because they knew as well as I what was going on, and there was really no time to discuss anything. It was a horrible, survival-of-the-fittest moment. I took a deep breath and braced myself. Our car came off the tracks and leaned to the right. I felt a downward surge. But as suddenly as the pandemonium had begun, we ground to a halt. Our car was still mostly upright in the gravel, and none of the guys had gone off the roof.

What had seconds before been an indescribable din was now an eerie quiet. The only noises came from the spinning wheels of the cars that lay on their sides or were upside down. In a few seconds they, too, were silent. The dust in the air was heavy but settled quickly. None of us said a word for a few seconds, but then we all abruptly came back to life. We scrambled to the ladder and climbed down to survey the wreckage below.

"Get your backpack!" Willie barked at me. We hustled to our seats, grabbed our travel bags, and jumped out of the train. I thought it odd that many of the Bolivian passengers were still sitting calmly in their seats, leaning to compensate for the angle of the train car, and appeared relatively unperturbed by what had just happened. Riding inside, they had not seen what we had and probably had no idea of the extent of the damage or of the danger they had been in.

Willie, the Swiss guys, and I stayed together, more or less as a little group, climbing through the wreck and examining the twisted, smoldering junk pile that moments before had been the train. It became apparent that the first cars had carried no passengers so, colossal mess though it was, at least no one was injured or dead. We made our way forward, each of us pausing to inspect whatever piqued our curiosity. We ended up near the front where we could see that the four men on the crew had shut the engine off, climbed down onto the tracks, and were standing around pointing and talking. The engine, it seemed, was fine, sitting squarely on the tracks, as was the flat car immediately behind it. Directly behind that was a total disaster.

The mechanic and the engineer seemed to be focused on the electrical cables and the hydraulic and pneumatic lines that were stretched and twisted between the unharmed flat car and the following derailed car. They were examining everything very closely, talking quickly and using lots of hand gestures. One of them climbed up into the cab and returned with a few large, primitive tools, and they appeared to set about trying to disconnect the one car from the other. Willie nudged me with his elbow.

"I know exactly what these guys are doing," he whispered loudly. "They are going to disconnect this thing right here, jump back into the engine, fire it up, and take off. That's what they're doing. They're going to just leave all these people here. And I tell you what, if they do that, I'm jumping onto that flat car, and wherever they go, I'm going with them."

I tried to reassure him that no train official would ever do such a thing, but he was adamant.

"Uh, yes they would," he insisted. "And when they do, jump on. In fact, let's tell Pablo and Steffen and the rest of the guys now so they're ready too."

We told the others but their dismissive responses made me think they didn't believe a word of it. Less than a half hour later, the final connection popped loose and without so much as even looking at us, the captain and his crew climbed back into the engine and started it up with a huge burst of black smoke.

"What did I tell you?" Willie said as he threw his backpack onto the flat car and climbed on. I followed, as did the other Swiss guys, but Peter quickly announced that he didn't have his pack with him. It was still back in the passenger car. We all yelled at him at once to go get it. Snapped to his senses, he turned and bolted back down the tracks, climbing, jumping, and scrambling through the debris. He disappeared from view and just then the train started to move.

Old-fashioned trains accelerate very slowly. This train probably was good for a top speed of thirty-five miles per hour and most likely needed several minutes to get up to that speed. But pulling no weight except one empty flat car, it started to move out at a relatively smart pace. As we hit three or four miles per hour, Peter reappeared way back in the distance, doing a hundred-meter, high-hurdle dash through the havoc. In a few moments we were up to five or six miles per hour. Peter was gaining on us in spite of our steady increase in speed, and he broke through into the clearing, past the last of the wreckage just as we were up to eight or nine miles per hour. There was a brief moment when we were sure he would prevail, but just when he had given us that hope, the train picked up yet more speed. Even though he was now only ten yards behind us, he was going all out and his speed exactly matched ours. Cheer and yell as we might, two or three miles per hour faster on our part and it was all over. Peter had failed to reach us and was slowing to a walk. A feeling of helplessness set in as we watched him double over and put his hands on his knees to catch his breath after his sprint, and someone yelled, "Follow the tracks!"

CHAPTER 12

THE SHACK

We cruised along briskly for about fifty miles. By now, sunburn was becoming a significant problem and we all positioned ourselves to minimize our exposure. I noticed that the noise from the engine suddenly changed pitch, and we began a leisurely slowdown. Within a quarter of a mile the train stopped and I heard the engine shut off. Without the breeze from the forward motion, the stillness of the hot, humid air was almost unbearable. And after days of the same loud clatter, the silence sounded strange and out of place. We could hear only bird noises and the ruckus made by the train crew as they disembarked. We, too, jumped down off the flat car and by unspoken agreement, clustered around in a huddle wondering what would happen next. It was then that

I first noticed we had parked alongside a parallel set of tracks that extended for a couple hundred yards in either direction, and at each extreme, blended back into the single set of tracks we had been on all along. I also noticed that the crew was heading to what looked like an old, but solid-looking shack off to the side of the tracks. It was small, about thirty feet wide, twelve or fifteen feet deep, and it had windows on both sides of the front door. There was no front porch of any sort, but the roof overhung the front fascia and other walls by a foot or two. The sides and the back of the rustic structure were overgrown with jungle. If there were any other windows or doors, they weren't visible because, except for the clean front, the extremely dense foliage had almost consumed the building.

As the train crew neared the entrance, our little huddle broke up and we walked in the direction of the shack to meet up with them. They gave us a quick, nervous glance and hurried their pace. The lead guy got out some keys and quickly opened the door. He entered, let the three other guys in, and then slammed the door. We arrived a few seconds later, but none of us had any ideas about what to do next. Willie stepped forward and knocked. There was no answer. He knocked again. Still no answer. Then he raised the ante and slammed his fist into the door.

"Maybe they heard that one," he said. We knew they had heard us all along, but it wasn't until after the potent thud that a voice from inside finally asked us what we wanted. Willie did the talking for us.

"Can we come in?" he asked.

"No," came the answer.

One of the Swiss guys mentioned that right before the door slammed shut, he had seen that they had chairs and cots and bottled water in there, and we surmised they also had basic food supplies too. Willie tried again.

"Can you please give us some water?" he asked. Again came the dreaded answer.

"No."

"Please, we are burning up out here, and you have shade and water in there," Willie pleaded. "You need to help us." Again, the answer was simple.

"No."

As our hopes sank, our tempers rose. Willie, in particular, was not going to take no for an answer, at least not without a fight. He pounded his fist against the door again, shaking the whole front of the building. Then he lambasted them for their total lack of any sense of responsibility for the predicament we were in. After that he started yelling insulting little jokes through the front door.

"How does one become a train official in Bolivia? You flunk the test!" he shouted. "What do you have to do to become a train employee in Bolivia? You have to become a certified idiot!"

Finally, Willie told us that he would rip the door right off its hinges and help himself to the water and shelter before putting up with this too much longer. First, however, he gave the men inside fair warning. He slammed his fist into the door even harder than before and announced quite clearly that he was coming through, with or without their permission.

I then heard a very distinct sound from within, one that cannot be mistaken for any other sound in the world. It was the cocking of a pump shotgun. We all recognized it and cleared away from the door fearing they would shoot right through it. No shot rang out, but a stern voice from within did.

"Tenemos una escopeta!"

They had a gun. Furthermore, the voice continued, they would shoot and kill anyone who tried to damage the shack, or enter it. Willie refused to acknowledge defeat.

"You may have won this one, but it's not over yet!" he countered.

We retreated a short distance and searched around for any form of shelter, especially from the burning sun. I noticed there was shade under the flat car of the train, so I squatted down and went under there to check it out. Unfortunately the area was extremely oily and smelly, and the heat under there seemed worse than ever, so I abandoned that idea. The afternoon was waning, and for the first time, the thought hit me that we may very well be outside all night, completely unprotected.

I had never thought of a jungle as something that has its own special voice, but as it slowly became dark, there was a strange evolution in the sounds emanating from the thicket. With no mechanical clatter to overpower the night's subtle noises, it seemed as though we entered a new world as darkness fell.

THE SUNBAKED TIN CAN

Entire ecosystems quieted down and their nocturnal counterparts emerged. To a handful of foul smelling, half-starved travelers, this meant again fending off aggressive flying and crawling things that literally wanted to eat us. By this point we were just over three days into the trip and had gone the last forty-eight hours without food or water. We were ravaged by extreme thirst, hunger, and sleep deprivation.

We all mulled about the area and one by one, each of us settled into his own little custom-built nest, some of us expending more time and energy than others to make a comfortable spot for the night. Dialogue was limited. We were all more or less in the same condition, and there was an unspoken agreement not to bother each other with trivial problems. I curled up on the rocks out along the side of the tracks and drifted in and out of sleep. I woke up periodically in order to crush to death various things I felt crawling up my pants leg, into my socks or shoes, or down my shirt. The worst were the ones trying to tunnel their way into an ear or up my nose, or the ones trying to set up shop in an armpit or claw their way between my lips to get into my mouth. Certain bugs seemed to want to nest in my hair, while others tried to dig their way into any number of places on my body I usually don't give much thought to. Reality and reverie became indistinguishable as the night dragged on. When the sound of shrill laughter startled me, I sat up, looked around, and saw that it was morning.

Willie and the others were talking and joking around. I got up and joined them and again heard the shriek that originally had awakened me—it was Hans whose laughter, normal a few days ago, had become a high-pitched cackle. They were all comparing their bloody, swollen bites and smashed dead creatures. An intriguing variety of wounds could be found all over each of our bodies. Fortunately, we were able to find some humor in the carnage, although maybe the laughter was a survival mechanism.

We soon noticed that although the shack had become a hostile place, the low, rising sun cast a long, welcome shadow between the front of the shack and the tracks. We quietly walked over to the shack and lined up shoulder-to-shoulder across the front of it, facing the tracks, our backs to the shack. We did not want to do anything to alarm the guy inside with the shotgun, but the shade was receding fast as the sun rose, and we needed to take advantage of it while we could.

CHAPTER 13

THE CHICKEN

I was at the far right end of our lineup. Our group was quietly enjoying the shade when about fifty yards down the tracks to the east, in the direction of Brazil, I thought I saw something moving. I wiped the sweat out of my eyes as best I could and tried to focus. Indeed, there was something moving. In another moment, I realized that it was a chicken. I glanced to my left at the others and saw that, other than Hans, right next to me, none of them had noticed it yet. I nudged Hans with my elbow as I pointed down the tracks, and he acknowledged our find with a nod and a smile. Then we both let the others in on what we had seen. A rush of enthusiasm overcame us as we all agreed that it certainly was a chicken, and that we might be able to make a meal out of it.

"In Switzerland, I used to work on a farm in the summers," Hans quickly volunteered. "I think I know how to catch that chicken."

No one protested and in no time we were encouraging him to go down the tracks and get it. Hans sauntered away from us trying his best to be stealthy. He walked sort of sideways as he approached the chicken, as if that would make him less visible. He didn't seem very sneaky to me, but I figured he knew something from the farm that I didn't know. When he was within about twenty feet, he slowed his pace and began to act as if he had no interest in the chicken but just happened to be standing around nearby. He continued to do this for some minutes, inching ever closer in little steps that I assumed were meant to appear unintentional and non-threatening to the chicken. It looked as though he was also quietly whistling a tune, as if that would help his proximity appear less deliberate. Then he lunged. With all his might and main, he threw himself full-on—arms outstretched, fingers clawing the air—right at the chicken. He crashed heavily and clumsily onto the rocks, grunting and groaning as he frantically groped and squirmed. Then he quickly looked all around, knowing he had failed but hoping he could still save the effort with a little luck. From our perspective he looked ridiculous, and it was obvious that the chicken had handily outmaneuvered him. The chicken had run straight into the jungle at the first sign of his primitive little pounce. He stood up and dusted himself off, as if it mattered, and dejectedly walked back toward us. And man, did we give him a hard time.

"I used to work on a farm. Maybe now I'm almost as smart as a chicken," said Klaus, the mockery heavy in his tone.

"My name is Hans and my brain is growing. Soon it will be as big as the brain of a chicken!" quipped Steffen.

"Should we call you 'Farmer' or 'Chicken' from now on instead of Hans? Which one do you prefer?" Pablo asked sarcastically.

With each new dig came a burst of laughter from the rest of us. Hans tolerated the teasing for a minute or so and then walked away and resumed his place in the shade.

"OK, you can shut up now. I think that's enough," he shot in our general direction, although he sounded more humored than angry.

Klaus chirped out a surprisingly good clucking sound that sent us all into another round of laughter, and then we each took turns doing our best to imitate a rooster's morning crow. Hans was actually grinning as he shook his head and tried to act like he wasn't amused. We chuckled as we tossed around a few snide chick and hen remarks but soon we quieted down. As we stood around trying to get over the loss of our meal, Hans sat quietly alone, forlornly looking down the tracks. Then all of a sudden he jumped to his feet and pointed into the distance.

"Hey, the chicken is back!" he abruptly announced. "This time I'll get it for sure."

Since the rest of us knew nothing about chickens and our resident farmer at least claimed to, we accepted his offer. We even pointed out that if he caught it this time, we would never again mention his failed first attempt. So off Hans went, again walking sort of sideways and again slowing near the chicken and pretending to putter around disinterestedly.

Again he pounced with full force, leaping and diving like a swimmer entering a pool for a race. Again he belly-flopped heavily onto the rough, filthy gravel, all the while groping and flailing, blindly hoping to suddenly grasp feathers instead of air. And yet again, he missed badly. He walked back toward us, this time a bit more aggressively, as if to let us know not to start with the put-downs, but again, we let him have it.

"Knock it off," he protested. "This time, I've got it nailed down. I have it all worked out. Those two tries were just for practice. You'll see," he insisted.

We barely let him get another word in as we started back into the chicken jokes, but Hans eventually got through to us that he had learned something significant.

"Just listen," he implored. "I was watching very carefully, and both times the chicken ran away from me along exactly the same path. And both times it went into the jungle at exactly the same spot. All we need to do now is wait until it comes out again, then one of us hides in the bushes right where the chicken always runs. Then I will go out to catch it and repeat the same method as before, and the chicken will run right into the hands of the guy who is waiting on the escape path. And then it's meal time."

We had to admit that for someone with such poor chicken-catching skills, he had thought things out rather well. Klaus quickly volunteered for the actual catch in the bushes, and in a few moments, Hans was ready for the set-up.

Within ten minutes, our prospective lunch was happily pecking around near the tracks, exactly as before. Hans then showed Klaus exactly where the chicken would run to, and where to hide in the underbrush. Then, with the accustomed crab-walk and casual whistling, the farmer-turned-secret-agent-man meandered as innocently and inconspicuously as possible to within a few yards of the chicken. As expected, he flung himself at the bird, this time putting much less heart into it. It all played out perfectly. The chicken ran into the jungle and disappeared. For a moment there was silence. Just as we were beginning to wonder if something had gone wrong, Klaus emerged from the bushes smiling from ear to ear and carrying a very angry chicken by the neck. We all burst into applause, especially Hans. As Klaus neared us, dangling the outsmarted fowl from his clenched fist, I opened my big mouth.

"What are you going to do with it now?" I asked.

I watched in horror as he promptly did with the chicken's neck exactly what one would do to crack a whip. Of course, the neck snapped, and then Klaus let the chicken go. It hit the ground and ran around aimlessly, flipping over, tumbling, flapping frantically, and even getting airborne for short distances before crashing again, feathers flying the whole time.

I felt really bad, as if the whole morbid display was my fault, even though I knew that wasn't true. I also got over the trauma very quickly as we all worked together to gather sticks and build a fire. Hans got out a Swiss army knife and made quick work of preparing our fine feathered friend for consumption. In no time, we were squatting in a circle around a nice little fire, each of us with his own stick and a skewered chunk of chicken, roasting the meat like marshmallows. We had divided up the spoils into roughly equal parts, and as soon as the various pieces appeared even remotely cooked, we devoured them.

THE SUNBAKED TIN CAN

Before we had downed the last of the apportioned morsels, our attention was diverted to what sounded like a hysterical person in the distance. Sure enough, standing near the tracks, just about where the chicken had been, there stood a woman. She was dressed in garb the likes of which I had never seen before, and she appeared to be yelling at us. She was waving her arms, gesticulating wildly, and seemed quite upset. We did a quick check among ourselves to see if anyone knew what she was saying, and although our group was proficient in seven or eight different languages, not a one of us could understand her. She finished her rant, pivoted around, and headed straight into the jungle, near the place where the chicken had fled.

"Good, shut up!" Klaus said.

And then, just when we thought she was gone, she returned, holding a live chicken by the neck. With a stylistically different but equally effective quick arm movement, she snapped the chicken's neck and flung it onto the ground in front of her. I watched the sickening display again as the hapless chicken went haywire, frantically flopped around, and finally expired. The woman then stomped off into the jungle again.

"Good, more chicken!" Klaus said, sounding downright flippant.

As we tried to reach a group consensus as to whether we should simply retrieve the second chicken and eat it too, the crazed woman appeared again. She looked directly at us and resumed her screaming and shouting, all the while grasping another live chicken by the neck. Once more, just as she appeared to be finished venting, she deftly snapped the chicken's neck.

This was starting to make some of us feel a little nervous. Personally, I had visions of her husband charging out of the forest any second, poison darts at the ready. I imagined his wife then ordering him to do to us, the equivalent of what she was doing to the chickens. The hyped-up woman stormed off into the bush again, and we quickly agreed that someone had to go talk with her.

"Steffen, you're twenty-six. That's old like her," Klaus said boldly. "And besides, you speak at least five languages and the rest of us sure as hell don't know what she's saying. You go talk to her!"

If Steffen didn't want the job, we overwhelmed him before he could put up a fight. We all chimed in and supported Klaus, especially his idea that, among us, Steffen was closest to the age of the unhinged woman. Therefore, we figured, he could best relate to her. He reluctantly agreed.

We watched with trepidation as Steffen headed to where the mystery woman had last been seen. When she came out of the jungle again, as infuriated as ever, she had yet another chicken at the ready. Steffen slowed his approach to show her he meant no aggression, and she held her ground. They squared off at a distance that would allow conversation without the need to shout, and we could tell that our ambassador was really trying. The irate woman listened to him and answered with lots of emotion, and as the seconds ticked by, they actually seemed to connect. In short order, she went back into the jungle without killing the chicken, and Steffen walked back to talk to us. Diplomacy, it seemed, had prevailed.

THE CHICKEN

The woman was angry because we had killed her chicken. Soothed by the efforts of our envoy, however, she had made us an offer. She would make soup out of the ones she had killed if we would pay for the soup and pay for the first chicken we had stolen. Of course, Steffen had agreed. It seemed that in no time, we would be eating like kings. Within a few minutes the lady reemerged from the jungle, this time accompanied by a group of young children, carrying between them a large pot, utensils, and a variety of vegetables.

The kids fetched the spent chickens, a fire was quickly built, and we paid up the paltry, agreed-upon sum. In a little over an hour, we were being fed a delicious meal. The kids had become very friendly by this point and manifested an avid curiosity about almost everything we said or did. I was convinced that they found all the dead bugs clinging to our shirts most amusing. In a little while their mother said something to them that we didn't understand, and they ran into the jungle and returned with several faded, dented, unopened cans of still-pressurized, hot beer. We immediately assigned Steffen the job of asking how many more they had, and they enthusiastically retrieved their entire stash—the equivalent of three or four six-packs. We purchased the whole lot and did not waste any time drinking it. I had a bad feeling about slamming down a lot of hot beer all at once when I was so thirsty and dehydrated, so I drank only two. When Hans saw that I was saving one of my cans of beer, he talked me into selling it to him. The watery soup had boiled long enough to be germ-free, and I had eaten my fill of it. My hunger pains were gone and my thirst, for the moment, was quenched.

CHAPTER 14

THE FONT

I felt the mild effects of the alcohol as I searched around for shade. Near the edge of the jungle, I found a large-leafed, low plant that I could squat under to stay mostly out of the sun. The Swiss guys, now quite happy, engaged the kids in a game of soccer. They had no ball, so instead they used what looked like an old coconut, still in the oblong husk. It was useless as a soccer ball and didn't roll any better than an American football. Yet they all ran back and forth, yelling excitedly at anything that remotely resembled a kick, an interception, or an imaginary goal. As I watched the madness, I soon found myself very thirsty again and noticed that one of the kids had exited the soccer game, run into the jungle, and returned several minutes later covered with fresh mud. A short while later, another little boy did the same. I figured that where there was mud, there was water, so I decided to follow one of the boys to see where they were going.

Just then another kid, whose mud had dried into a blanket of crust, charged off to renew the moisture, and I followed. He ran quickly, snaking through the bush much more adroitly than I, and soon we came to a small clearing. Sure enough, there was a large mud puddle, with a very low-pressure, burbling spring oozing water out of the ground right in the center. The kid ran into it, slipping, sliding, falling, and totally covering himself in fresh mud and water. Then he ran back out to the soccer game.

I waded into the mud circle and found the very center and the little source. It gently welled up an inch or so before spilling off and dissipating into its surroundings. I was ankle-deep in mud by then, but I didn't care. I desperately wanted to quench my thirst, but I also knew of the dangers of drinking contaminated water. In order to get my face down as close as possible to ground level to examine the spring and try to determine its purity, I attempted all sorts of distorted poses and balancing tricks. I was soon able to get my mouth almost to the surface of the water without falling over into the muck. In my deluded state, quenching my thirst suddenly seemed overwhelmingly more important to me than concerning myself with the consequences if the water was contaminated. The water didn't seem cloudy or smell like sewage, so I decided it was clean enough to drink. I puckered my lips out as far as they would go and slurped up the precious liquid, swallow after swallow.

Then I slogged my way back out of the viscous sludge and followed the trail through the dense overgrowth, back to the railroad tracks and the others. I saw a couple of my companions resting peacefully on the crude but level surface in front of the little cabin, and I joined them.

Our backs were against the rough, old building and we were chatting quietly when I heard a cry from Hans. He was most agitated and was urgently pointing down the tracks in the direction from where we had come. I had a look for myself, and there in the distance was the walking ghost of none other than Peter, the guy that had missed the train after it derailed.

He was trudging, slowly but with determination, right down the middle of the tracks and, by any reading of his body language, had not yet seen us. Several of the guys ran in his direction, calling out to him. He was slow to respond but eventually started acting like an adrenaline-spiked zombie. He had walked fifty miles in 110-degree heat with no food or water, and he looked like he was near death. As he approached, he seemed uncoordinated and punchy, and when he reached our little camp, he manifested severe sunburn and dehydration. But most troubling of all, the heat and exposure had swollen and cracked his lips so badly he couldn't move them to talk. He grunted a bit and gestured weakly to indicate that he was happy to see us. Privately, I wondered why he had not walked at night and slept during the day in the shade of the jungle foliage. I felt sure that that's what I would have done if I had been in his situation.

Our little group quickly teamed up to scrounge together what we could of the remaining soup and whatever other liquids we could muster. I told everyone about the little spring and obliged Steffen, who insisted on checking it out. I led him directly to it.

"There is no way you can drink that water," he said after a quick look at the small mire. "Who knows what horrible diseases are lurking in that mess."

"Well, I just drank quite a bit of it," I confessed. I pointed as I continued, "But I was right there in the middle where the water looks clean and even smells clean."

"Uh, well, it might not hurt you," he offered. "You're much better off than Peter. He's far too dehydrated for that water, but um, you'll probably be okay."

I wasn't sure what he meant by that but I didn't want to argue. When we returned, the children had informed their mother of the new arrival and she attended to getting him some soup. I found it ironic that we were so relieved and elated to have reunited with our lost buddy when, in fact, we were still more or less out in the middle of nowhere, with no end to our ordeal in sight.

CHAPTER 15

THE CRANE

After a short while, we heard a rumble in the distance that turned out to be a two-car train coming from the direction of our destination. We rejoiced at the prospect of help arriving and finally being able to continue on our journey. The train slowed to a stop and its crew climbed down and entered the little cabin. The rig was well equipped to fix broken machinery but the rescuers had not brought a single drop of water for us stranded passengers. The mood in our marooned group changed quickly as our initial sense of relief was overshadowed by broader feelings of disappointment and even anger at being treated so indifferently.

The rescue train obviously was outfitted to clear wreckage. Its chief feature was a crane with a massive hook that appeared to have been well used. Following a brief meeting of the minds in the cabin, a couple of the crew exited and got back aboard the crane-train, which then disappeared into the distance toward the wreck. We figured they would first rescue the other abandoned passengers and then we would soon be on our way. I briefly pondered what the others had been doing, and how they had fared. My mind went to the French girl, particularly since she appeared to have minimal luggage with her and, therefore, was most likely out of provisions. Many of the other train occupants, especially the locals, seemed to be traveling with every earthly thing they owned, including livestock, and I presumed they were making do. Images of specific individuals came to my mind, especially of one wide-eyed, terrified, elderly man, torn momentarily between running for his life empty-handed or bringing his belongings with him in his escape during the "cold-milk" incident. But I had enough worries of my own, and as darkness fell, I returned to the simple routine that had seen me through the previous nights.

Early the next morning, with some nourishment in our systems and the relative cool of the previous night fading fast, our group gathered in the shade next to the little barrack and anticipated the arrival of the rest of our fellow crash survivors. Instead, the lone crane contraption rumbled back toward us, stopped briefly, and then took off in the direction of Brazil. Two of the four occupants of the cabin soon fired up the train engine with the flat car and took off in reverse, toward the wreck. We did not feel it necessary to go along because we knew they had left a couple of guys in the little shed. As such, they would have to stop again on the way by, at which time we would jump on. About four hours later, along came our train. Other than the fact that it was now quite a bit shorter, it looked as though it had never been in an accident. It stopped, and we got on board along with the remaining crew. It was hard to believe, but we were back in the saddle again. It was just ten thirty and we had the whole day—and potentially lots of progress—ahead. I noticed the French woman, sitting in exactly the same seat, with exactly the same resolve not to talk to anyone, and any concern I might have had for her faded away.

Scarcely three hours later, quite a few passengers began gathering their belongings as if the ride would soon be over. I snapped out of my stupor and looked outside to see what was going on. The landscape had changed markedly. We were coming into a populated area, and I suspected that we were on the outskirts of Puerto Suarez—the end of the first leg of the trip. The train creaked and slowed to perhaps ten miles per hour. After a few minutes, we slowed down to a walking pace. I watched the passing scenery through the window to learn as much as I could even though we had no plans to visit the city. This stop was but a necessary transfer point along the path to great things in Rio.

As our train coasted to a stop, I noticed quite a few soldiers and a lot of military equipment outside. Just as in Santa Cruz, all the machine guns made me nervous. I tried to dismiss my fears and relax, but my effort was interrupted by loud shouts, the stomping of boots, and the shrieks people make when things suddenly get out of control.

CHAPTER 16

"MY TOWN"

I saw a flood of soldiers pour through the front entrance of our train car, and I spun around to see that the back entrance was being stormed too. A dozen or more soldiers were aggressively knocking people out of their way and charging toward the center of our car, weapons drawn, fingers on the triggers, bayonets slicing the air. Passengers dove back into their seats to allow the thundering assault to pass by. The two-pronged swat-team raid continued until it arrived at our little group. The camouflaged marauders hollered and thrust their rifle barrels into our faces and we were ordered to grab our things and shut up. In a matter of seconds, we were herded off the train. We were surrounded and marched across a flat dirt parking area, then ordered up onto the bed of a large, flatbed truck. The soldiers forced us to sit in a tight circle and face the center as they constantly jabbed us in the back with their weapons and yelled at us to shut up and not move. Then the truck whisked us away. After ten minutes of bouncing along a dusty, unpaved road, the truck ground to a sudden halt, and we were ordered to disembark. As I recovered from my cramped position, I saw that Willie, Pablo, the other Swiss Germans, and I were the only ones who had been nabbed, and that we were outside of what looked like a large prison.

We were rushed through several layers of tall, heavy gates, some topped with large coils of razor-sharp wire. In a series of well-practiced, perfectly synchronized movements, the outer gates of the fortress were opened for us and then slammed and locked behind us. We crossed about fifty yards of open lawn and then entered an enormous building. Our captors continued to loudly reiterate orders to hurry up and shut up as we traversed several long hallways and made a series of right and left turns. We then descended several flights of stairs and eventually found ourselves at the bottom of the last set of steps, in front of a large, heavy door. This was the end of the line. There were no more hallways, no more rights or lefts, and no more stairs.

We had been flooded with bright, fluorescent lights since entering the building, and even though we were almost certainly underground by this point, everything was still very well-lit. The small square landing at the bottom of our final descent was barely large enough to accommodate us as we stood, silently pressed together. A large soldier suddenly muscled his way through our midst, unlocked, and opened the door. Without a word, he shoved us through the opening and slammed the door shut. No one made a sound as we stood on the damp, dirt surface in the pitch darkness, without even the slightest idea of what we had done wrong. The air smelled like a mixture of death and an overused outhouse. The last noises we heard came from a series of deadbolts turning and locking one by one, sealing our fate.

My eyes watered and I fought off an explosive urge to vomit as I tried to get used to the smell. I plugged my nose and breathed through my mouth, used my shirt as a filter, and tried to imagine that things would get better. The rancid air was notably cooler than the outside air had been, and I reflected that my tortured, perspiration-drenched body might at least have a chance to cool down. I don't know why, but I desperately wanted to know how big the room was, and what shape it had. I tried my best but could not discern even the tiniest speck of light. Nor was there the remotest visual sign of any wall, floor, or ceiling, though I knew those things were surely there. As my eyes searched the black void in vain, I perceived the carefully controlled sound of our group's tense breathing as our thoughts raced and each of us engaged his own strategy for dealing with the stench, exhaustion, and raw fear. We all remained silent, scarcely moving a muscle, afraid to even whisper. I convinced myself early on that I must remain calm and not expend too much energy doing anything until, with time, my eyes became accustomed to the dark.

I have never felt so alone in the immediate presence of a handful of other people. Finally someone spoke. Very softly, very hesitantly, Pablo whispered.

"Does anyone know what the hell is going on?"

I had been waiting for this moment because I was sure that something must have been said in Spanish that I had not understood that would explain why we were being treated so badly. I knew that Willie understood the language quite well, and that at least two of the Swiss guys spoke Spanish fluently, but in the end no one had a clue why we had been arrested. We bickered aimlessly for a minute or two and agreed that our talking might be overheard and used against us in whatever they had in store for us next. The chatter had comforted most of us immensely, and we devised a strategy of returning to complete silence so we could listen for noises. The one exception was that the first person who could see anything was to quietly notify the rest of us.

Two hours later, it was still as dark as the inside of a buried coffin, and we had heard no discernible noises. We had kept utterly silent, as agreed, and I began to wonder how much longer I would be able to stand. I was tremendously fatigued, and the almost complete lack of sight and sound left me feeling disoriented.

Abruptly, we heard footsteps and then muffled voices as the deadbolts clattered. With no warning, the door was brutally kicked fully open. It narrowly missed a couple of us and slammed against the inside wall. A blinding flood of light poured in upon us and at the same instant, we were again jabbed in the ribs with rifles.

"*Ándale! Apúrense! Cállense!*"

We were loudly ordered to walk quickly, to stay tightly grouped, and to be silent. I was harshly pushed toward the stairs, and I stumbled but quickly recovered. I fought to adjust my eyes to the stunning brightness after being in the dark so long. We went up two flights of stairs, down a corridor, and made a few turns that were not leading us back the way we had come in. Finally, we were pushed into a large room. A soldier shouted at us.

"*Todas sus cosas allí! Todos ustedes allá!*"

The gunmen shoved us and pointed as they ordered us to place all of our belongings along the north wall and line up along the south wall, side by side, with our backs to the wall. I picked up on the visual cues and followed the lead of the others who understood Spanish and we all hastily complied.

The room was huge and perfectly square. It had no windows and only one door. The entire chamber—floor, ceiling, walls, and the one door—was impeccably clean, and painted a smooth, radiant, high-gloss white. There were dozens upon dozens of fluorescent lights covering nearly every square foot of the high ceiling, making the room intensely bright. The overpowering, sun-like luminescence stole any sense of privacy, real or imagined, and I felt like everyone in the room could see into my very thoughts. The thousands of watts served their masters well, penetrating and revealing us like so many amoebas in a drop of water under a powerful microscope. A lineup of five armed guards stood parallel to us and stared us down, trigger-fingers at the ready, watching every move we made. One broke out of formation and approached us. He singled out Steffen.

"Recoge tu mochila!" he ordered. *"A ver. Qué tienes?"*

Steffen understood. He was to walk across the room to the pile of our belongings, grab everything that was his, bring it to the middle of the room, and empty the backpack's contents.

We watched in silence as the items cascaded out of the backpack and thudded onto the hard, polished floor. Three of the guards went to the middle of the room and oversaw the emptying of the backpack while the other two watched us carefully. Two of the guards then proceeded to rummage through the items strewn about the floor. They broke apart any bars of soap they found, squeezed out the toothpaste, dumped out any bottles of liquids such as shampoo or cologne, and snapped all the pens and pencils in half. They held aloft any books they found, with the spine facing the ceiling and the pages dangling down, and then they thumbed harshly forward and backward through each book several times, tearing away whole pages in the process. Any loose piece of paper such as a bookmark, a phone number, or a personal note, fluttered down onto the mess below. The soldiers went through all of the clothing and any pockets they could find and finished their search by using a machete to expertly slice in half the heel of any spare pair of shoes or boots they found. Then they gave their "prisoner" a thorough body search and after that, ordered him to move the whole pile of clutter that had once been his precious possessions over to the west wall. He was then directed to walk back across the room and stand at attention, facing the center of the room, with his back to the east wall.

One by one, in a systematic and almost routine fashion, they searched each of us and all of our belongings. At one point I wondered if they would treat all of us as guilty if they found something illegal on only one of us. I dared not dwell on just how little I knew about my travel companions—I didn't even know their last names. When the last of us stood with his back up against the east wall, looking across to our tangled belongings, the soldiers exchanged a few brief words. With that, one of them marched briskly across the room and exited, slamming the door shut behind him. The others squared off and studied us, caressing their rifles and making it very clear who was the boss. Not two minutes later, the door burst open and in walked a hideously dressed, singularly repulsive human being. He chirped out a brief, shrill whistle, and gestured halfheartedly in the direction of the door with an uncoordinated wave of his left hand. Our guards had snapped to their finest, full-attention stance when he entered, and they responded to his command by running to the door and exiting the room within a few seconds.

He was short, maybe five foot five, very heavy-set, and bald. He wore no shirt and had a huge, hairy gut on which gravity had taken a very unforgiving toll. He wore a pair of tight, green polyester pants, pulled up as high as he could get them, and the pant legs ended halfway between his knees and his ankles. He had tight black socks that did not nearly reach to the bottom of the pant legs, exposing several inches of bare, hairy leg in the gap. On his feet, he wore tight, pointy-toed, black leather ankle boots with zippers where the laces would normally be. To me, they looked like something an elf would wear. He had an extremely hairy back, and from behind he looked half-animal. From the front, his oversized gut dominated the view. His belly button was difficult to see, as it hung several inches below the belt and aimed more toward the ground than forward. The side view had me wondering if the skin in the main crease near his beltline had seen any fresh air in years. His arms hung from their shoulder sockets like rigid, fake little stumps and seemed too small for his torso. His face was clean-shaven and blended smoothly into his shiny cranium, and he looked mean. He stood off to our extreme right near the door, and he eyed us up and down, silently intimidating us. It was nearly a hundred degrees in the room and his entire body dripped with perspiration.

He began to walk toward us like a large, menacing penguin. I soon came to see that, due to his immense gut, his center of gravity was no longer where it was supposed to be, and that if he didn't lean back while he ambled forward or stood still, he might lose his balance and topple over. As he approached from our right, I could hear him breathing heavily. He walked slowly past our lineup, with his left side to us. He stared straight ahead, not saying a word as he strutted, bird-like, within two feet of us. As he passed by me, I saw that he had a huge, chrome .45-caliber pistol. It was stuffed into the center of the back of his pants so the handle could be grabbed in an instant, and the large, heavy barrel was buried deeply into the netherworld of his backside.

He strode a pace or two past the end of our lineup, and then whirled 180 degrees around on his heel and strutted past us again. Once he was back to where he had started, he repeated his well-practiced rotation maneuver, and again walked by, uncomfortably close to us. He repeated this little routine for an agonizing five minutes in total silence. I lost count of how many times he passed by, but it did occur to me to grab his gun, yank it out, and blow his head off, all in one single, swift move. I actually saw the whole thing play out in my mind. With each passing, I grew more fearful that I would act on my idea out of uncontrolled impulse, so when he couldn't see me, I carefully slipped my hands behind my back and clasped them together, white-knuckling them so that I wouldn't do anything stupid. With a little more thought, I became convinced that his gun was not loaded, and that this whole exercise was designed to tempt one of us into grabbing it. Then he could feel justified treating us any which way he saw fit, for as long as he wanted. No, I would not fall for it, and I prayed none of my companions would either.

My thoughts were interrupted as he suddenly stopped his pacing near the middle of our group. He turned his back to us and walked five or six paces away, toward the center of the large room. Then he spun around to face us and stood almost frozen. His eyes were dark and empty, as if witnessing the unspeakable had left them hollow and dead. Any humor initially evoked by his clown-like attire had long since been coldly doused—this was a man to be feared. One by one he examined each of us as if he had special powers and could see into people's souls. He crossed his stubby little arms, rested them on his protruding abdomen, and finally spoke, in Spanish. Only later, when the others translated it for me, did I find out what he had said.

"The first thing you boys need to know is that this is *my* town. And I don't like you or your kind in my town," he said. After a long pause, he continued. "But today is your lucky day. I'm going to give you exactly five minutes to gather up all of your stuff, and my guards are going to walk you to the exit gate of this prison. And then you are going to get into a taxi and get the hell out of my town. And if I ever see you in my town again, I'll lock you up again, and the next time, you'll never get out. You've got five minutes. Hurry up!"

We scurried across the room, suspecting that we might be pawns in a perverse, no-win sting, and that we would be pounced upon any second and returned to the chamber of total darkness. Nevertheless, almost in a panic, we crammed random belongings into equally random backpacks, unconcerned with what was whose, and in two or three minutes we were being expeditiously escorted to the exit. We were soon outside of the building, and in another minute, outside the outermost gate—and free. We could barely contain our exuberance and nervous energy as we hailed an oncoming taxi. When the driver said he could take only four of us, we agreed that the Swiss guys, traveling as a group of four, should go first. Willie, Pablo, and I very quickly found another taxi, and were off.

CHAPTER 17

THE NEW LAW

The section of the Bolivian-Brazilian border we needed to cross had a very peculiar geography to it. On the Bolivian side was the town of Puerto Suarez, located ten or twelve miles west of the actual line that separated the two countries. On the Brazilian side was the town of Corumbá, situated nearly five miles east of the border itself. In between, there was a fifteen-mile stretch of swampy jungle—part forest, part bulldozed wasteland—with no infrastructure whatsoever. The only way to get from either city to the other was down a neglected dirt road, by taxi. Forty-five minutes and several thousand jarring potholes after we got into our taxi, we came upon the border itself. At that point we were getting close to Corumbá and in the distance, the no-man's land ended and the city began. There was the usual abundance of gun-toting young men in military garb and a reasonably orderly scene. Our Swiss friends had arrived a few minutes before us and were gathered together to exchange backpacks and belongings. We joined them, sorted through it all, and in theory each of us had his own things back. All smiles, we proceeded to the crossing area, passports at the ready.

The Swiss guys went first and crossed over with a minimum of formalities. Willie stepped up to the border guard, showed his passport, and was asked a question in Portuguese that he didn't understand. After repeating himself several times to no avail, the guard asked Willie to step aside. He then checked Pablo's passport and let him cross. When it was my turn, he asked me the same question he had asked Willie. Like Willie, I couldn't understand what he wanted.

"He is asking you for your visas," Steffen offered. He understood Portuguese and, having overheard the exchange, had walked back to help. We politely told the border guard through our translator that Americans did not need visas to enter Brazil. Indeed, we had checked before we had left. Not only had our guidebook specifically stated that Americans needed only a passport to enter Brazil, but we had also talked to Americans in Santa Cruz who had just been in Brazil, and they had assured us no visa was necessary. Our Swiss friend explained in his best Portuguese that we were sure we were not mistaken, and after digesting a brief tirade by the border guard, he translated to us that, yes, that was the way it had always been, but within the last twenty-four hours the law had changed. There was a new law, there was no mistake, and without visas, the two Americans were not going to enter Brazil under any circumstances. As soon as Pablo and the Swiss guys understood our situation, they decided to move on without us. As they piled into a taxi to the train station in Corumbá, they waved goodbye.

"See you in Rio!" Pablo called out.

The border guard terminated his exchange with us by firmly clarifying that the nearest Brazilian consulate where a visa could be obtained was back in Santa Cruz.

I couldn't believe what I was hearing. For a moment, everything went numb. Noise faded into the distance and the real world around me seemed fake, as though I were watching a movie. The defeat was crushing. The promise of a full stomach, a quenched thirst, a warm shower, clean clothes, and freedom from torment by man and nature, had been within inches of our grasp. And then in an instant it was ruthlessly snatched away. Although physically decimated, I had remained mentally strong until this last slap in the face. Now, a deep fear crept through me and I was at a total loss as to what to do next. Willie, with his keen understanding of human nature, looked at me and sensed the vacuum in my core. He beckoned me to approach him closely and leaned in as if to whisper a secret.

"I've got a plan," was all he said.

Pulled back from the edge of a foreboding precipice, I gathered my wits and focused. Willie explained that these sorts of things happened all the time and that the cultures in South America had built-in checks and balances for just such occasions. He tried to ease my mind by suggesting that when all else failed, it was considered socially acceptable in Latin America to pay people for favors. He explained that although in the United States this was considered bribery, where we were it was simply looked at as paying an agreed-upon price in exchange for goods or services. The trick here, he explained, was to get the amount right and present the business deal in such a way as to never insult anyone.

We would wait until the border guards were relaxed and appeared to be stress-free. Then we would offer to pay them to let us in if we promised to go directly to Rio to get the visas. In this way, we could simply be treated in Rio as though we had already been in Brazil without a visa when the law passed. After all, wasn't that the case with perhaps thousands of Americans? Surely there was some amnesty period for Americans trapped in the middle of Brazil with no visa to make their way to the nearest large city and secure the proper paperwork. If the border guard would fudge the facts just a little, for the proper fee, of course, both parties could end up very happy with the deal.

Willie waited for the right moment and I quietly stood by while he took a shot at it. After a lively exchange with the guard, he came back to me and reported the result.

"No, they won't go for it," he said. "That's usually the way it is with a brand new law. Enforcing it makes them feel important for now. In a few weeks or months, they'll be open to negotiating, but they won't budge now."

As despair set in on me again, Willie suggested that we wait until the work shift ended for the guys who wouldn't let us in, and then give the next batch of guards a try. Darkness had fallen by the time the new work crew was in place, and I had lost track of what time it was or how many hours had gone by. Willie again approached the border agents with all the persuasiveness he could muster while I waited and hoped. After ten minutes of finagling, he returned to me and said all hope was lost—we would not be entering Brazil.

The hunger, thirst, lack of sleep, filth, and new emotional low seemed to hit me all at once. I felt like I was in a bad dream. The sense of hopelessness and desperation was profound. I had been depleting my reserves for so long, I wasn't sure if I even had any adrenaline left. I started complaining to Willie about how big our problems were, and he unknowingly convinced me I was right without saying a word, because the look in his eyes had changed since the last defeat. We needed to do something fast, but I had no idea where to start. I tended to focus on the small, immediate problems at hand, but Willie had already begun to plan on a macro level. I was blathering incoherently about our predicament when he squared off in front of me, grabbed me by both shoulders, and looked me straight in the eyes.

"Look," he said, "what we need to do is take a taxi back into Puerto Suarez, stock up on some food and water, and get on the train back to Santa Cruz. Period. We sure as hell can't stay in Puerto Suarez and it doesn't have an airport. As horrible as it may sound, that train is our only way out of this mess. Besides, if we just had enough food and water and some sleep, things wouldn't seem so bad."

I knew he was right.

CHAPTER 18

THE STRIKE

We were drained to the core but we had a new, tangible goal. We walked a short distance to the dirt road from Puerto Suarez where the taxis gathered to wait for customers fresh from Brazil. We were accosted by shouting, waving drivers vying for our business and we quickly picked one. It was ten forty-five and long since dark, and we knew the ride would last nearly an hour and cost us about two dollars. I tried to relax, but the radio was blaring eighty percent static and twenty percent awful music. The potholes jounced us mercilessly every which way, and the air inside the old car was filled with dust, but our driver was skilled and knew the road well. He worked the curves and small uphill and downhill passes like a pro and seemed very efficient at his trade. I tried not to speculate as to when the next train would leave for Santa Cruz, or how long we would have to hide from the roving soldiers in their jeeps. We had no guarantee whatsoever that we would be able to successfully slip into and out of town unnoticed.

About an hour into our taxi ride, I began to wonder why we were not there yet. I told myself that it was dark and that we were not going as fast as we had during the day. And yet the ride dragged on and on. I checked my watch and realized something was wrong. We were an hour and twenty minutes into a trip that had taken about half that long just eight or nine hours earlier, and we were going faster than we had in the afternoon. Willie, even with no watch, also was aware that something wasn't right. I told him how long we had been riding.

"I thought so," he said. "I know exactly what this guy is doing, and I'm not in the mood for it right now. He thinks we just crossed the border from Brazil and have no idea how long this ride should last. So this joker is going to drive us around for a couple of hours and then try to charge us, like, ten times what the normal fare should be. I've seen this move before."

Willie was sitting on the driver's side in the back seat and, with no warning, he leaned forward and grabbed the taxi driver's right shoulder with a crushing grip and yelled something into his ear in Spanish. Then he sat back and translated for me.

"I told him if he doesn't have us at the train station in Puerto Suarez in five minutes, I am going to kill him, throw his body out the window, and drive the car there myself. Let's see what happens now."

The driver sped up, mumbling and cursing to himself, and started to push our speed to the point where he was probably damaging the car. Willie mentioned that in spite of the darkness, he was sure we had been down this same stretch of road before. Within two minutes, the driver braked hard, swerved to the right, drove up to the top of a little knoll, crested the hill, and then swooped down, right into town. In two more minutes, we were at the train station.

"Grab all of our stuff and get out of the car with it," Willie said firmly. "Then go a little ways down the sidewalk and get away from the car."

Willie sounded dead serious and I robotically did as he said. He got out of the car and approached the driver's window to pay. As expected, the driver wanted something like twenty dollars. Willie threw about three dollars through the window and into the man's lap. This was far more than our afternoon fare had been. Then the taxi driver began to protest, but Willie wasn't going to have any of it.

"Three dollars is more than enough," Willie interrupted. "If you want more, it's right here in my pocket. Just get out of the car and take it from me. But be warned, if you step out of that car, I'm going to take your head off."

I learned a few choice Spanish swear words as the little car zoomed off noisily into the night.

Relieved that our plan was working, we headed to the ticket booth. In most Latin American towns the train station is a hub of activity almost twenty-four hours a day. Even after midnight, when a town is all but shut down for the night, it's the one place where the ubiquitous homeless people, taxis, and street vendors are usually still milling about. But this station was eerily vacant and quiet. Something about the scene was just not right. As we approached the ticket counter, it all became clear. With each step we took, slowly but steadily, the large, dimly lit handwritten sign came into view, and one by one, the words on it broadcast the dreaded message for all eyes to see: *"El Ferrocarril Está En Huelga Hasta Tiempo Indeterminado."* I knew something was terribly wrong even before Willie translated it for me: "All Trains On Strike Until Further Notice."

Again, I needed to tap into reserves that were long ago spent. And again, I looked to Willie for strength. In a way, I felt he owed it to me for having gotten me into all this. I wasn't sure if I had any resilience left, so my only hope was that he did. At this point, things were so bleak and so many things had gone wrong that it all seemed almost unreal. My imagination and emotions had lost their bearings and were swirling as one, and it even briefly occurred to me to try to find some demented humor in our awful predicament. Unfortunately, however, we were not in a dream, and the outcome did matter. So Willie and I huddled together and concluded that if we used our heads, we would find a way out of the quagmire we were in. We then started to brainstorm. We decided to find lodging in the least likely place our obese little nemesis from the prison would send his goons to find foreigners to harass. We figured his minions would be searching in and near the more expensive hotels, restaurants, and tourist cafes in town, so we would lie low in a place patronized only by locals. We moved to where we could read our guidebook under the brightest of the station's feeble, flickering lights and began to look for the cheapest hotels in all of Puerto Suarez.

It was well after midnight, yet jeeps full of marauding young soldiers were still out raising hell. The jeeps had swivel-mounted machine guns on them, and the drunk, rowdy recruits would speed around town, terrorizing citizens and ravaging the infrastructure with absolute impunity. Before long, we would learn that it was common for them to open fire on anything they thought was fun to shoot, including cats and dogs. Around the clock, gunfire could be heard popping sporadically in the distance. We hid when we heard one of the jeeps speeding toward the train station. It slowed down as its occupants visually swept the area and then took off again in a blast of unmuffled exhaust noise. When the jeep was gone we decided to take a taxi to a lowly, F-rated hotel where, according to our guidebook, a room for two went for sixty cents a night.

A taxi appeared in the distance and fortunately kept sputtering in our direction until we could get its attention. We jumped in, gave the driver the name and address of the hotel we wanted, and asked him if he could take us there.

"I could take you that place, but staying there would not be a good idea," he warned. "I know of much better hotels than that one. I'll take you to one of the better ones."

Willie firmly told him not to do that and to just take us to the one we had indicated. The man continued to protest that he knew of far better accommodations and assured us that we would thank him later for saving us from our own ignorance. Willie again resorted to the shoulder-grab death grip and a loud, threatening voice. He ordered the driver to take us where we wanted to go—or else. The driver was very apologetic and he sped up and nervously fidgeted with the radio knobs as he drove us to our requested destination. When he dropped us off a short while later, we paid him generously and he sheepishly thanked us before driving away. It was nearly one in the morning. In the vague glow of one dim, distant streetlight, and in the serene silence of a sleeping, semi-residential neighborhood, we verified that we were on the right street and at the correct address. Then Willie shattered the quiet with a firm knock on the door.

At first there was no answer, so he knocked again. Subtly, but then more distinctly, we heard noises from within. In a minute or two, a very old, soft-spoken gentleman appeared.

"How can I help you?" he politely asked.

"Do you have a room for two tired travelers?" Willie responded.

The man gestured to us to enter. He led us along a dark path he had memorized probably many years before. We followed closely and soon entered his small, cluttered office. He turned on a lamp.

"How long do you want to stay?" he asked quietly.

"We don't know," Willie answered. "Maybe a week."

"How about if we discuss it tomorrow?" the old man suggested.

We paid for three nights and he led us to our room, explaining along the way where we could find the toilets, showers, and laundry-washing facilities. Then he handed us the key and walked away. We entered the clean, small room and saw two beds, an overhead light, a little table with a lamp and two chairs, and a window that looked out onto the central courtyard area. We agreed on which bed was whose. I immediately dropped down onto mine, fully clothed, with my shoes and the light still on, and passed out for the next sixteen hours.

CHAPTER 19

THE FROG

I woke up and opened my eyes but I was almost too stiff to move. I had lost nearly a day in a semi-comatose state, but I felt as though I had finally relaxed a bit. It was sweltering in the unventilated little room as I sat up in the bed and noticed that Willie was gone. I groped for my watch and saw that it was about five o'clock in the afternoon. I hobbled to the door, opened it and stepped out into a wall of heat, humidity, and brilliant sunlight. I quickly retreated back into the less hostile, dim interior of the room and tried to remember exactly where I was and how I had gotten there. In a few moments, Willie burst in and seemed very enthusiastic. He had reconnoitered the area and had a report.

THE FROG

It seemed he had found a new friend in the form of a pudgy little eleven-year-old street vendor with a superb inventory of snacks. The boy normally operated his portable vending stand on the sidewalk next to a nice park, directly across the street from our hotel. Willie had sampled the kid's wares and subsequently purchased nearly everything. The young man had done two weeks worth of business in five minutes and, learning where Willie "lived," had moved his entire enterprise to just outside our hotel for his and Willie's future convenience. Best of all, there was a first-rate mom-and-pop grocery store within three minutes walking distance of our hotel, and Willie already had procured some bottled water and basic foodstuffs. I was terribly dehydrated and immediately drank an entire liter of water. That was a great relief, but Willie's news was not all good.

The military jeeps continued to roam the streets, revving their engines and showing off their horsepower, their firepower, and their unchecked authority. After our experience in the prison, we had good reason to be fearful of them, but Willie pointed out that even the locals also seemed afraid and ran for their lives whenever a jeep turned a corner and raced down the street. We snacked on some delicious but hard bread, nondescript cheese, and bottled water. We discussed the fact that we had everything we really needed now and agreed that if going outside meant jeopardizing our freedom and maybe even our lives, it wasn't worth it. So Willie and I resolved in earnest, right then and there, not to go out again, except after dark. Other than to get food and water at night and to go to the train station when the strike was over, we would hole up in our room, keep the curtains closed, and hide.

The first few days were uneventful. Powerful afternoon rainstorms began and ended at the same time every day and dumped almost an inch of warm rain onto the town. We did our laundry and showered with rainwater caught in basins on the roof—leaves, debris, bird droppings, and mosquito larvae included. Above all, we established an eating, drinking, and sleeping routine that gradually replenished our starved bodies and drained spirits. We played cards, shared travel stories, and passed the time easily in our humble safe house.

THE FROG

The door to our room opened onto a traditional central patio area that Willie and I deemed safe. The patio was well-tended and featured trimmed shrubbery, small patches of lawn, potted plants, and benches. It also was decorated with a variety of colorful statues and porcelain figurines, such as dogs, cats, donkeys, frogs, and ducks. Several days into our stay, I left our room to wash some clothes in the hotel's outdoor laundry sink. I carried my clothes and some soap across the central garden area and began my task. I looked around as I worked the filthy attire against a scrub brush and, glancing to my left, I noticed an unusually well-crafted frog figurine. It was clearly a carved sculpture, as it was nearly as large as a bowling ball, but it had a color and detail to it that earned it a second look. As I drained the basin and refilled it for a second round of laundry scrubbing, I couldn't help but fix my gaze on the frog. Among all the kitsch at the hotel, this frog was different. It was so well done that the traditional glaze, designed to look like moisture, did not shine or reflect and looked quite real. I was captivated. I convinced myself that the clothing could benefit from a few minutes of soaking and left my station to walk over to the frog. The closer I got, the more real it appeared. When I was quite near I got down on my hands and knees and cautiously moved my face closer and closer. From no less than twelve inches away, I studied the splendid creature, amazed that something so detailed could be fake. And then it blinked.

I was so startled I slipped on the cobblestone pavement as I recoiled. My first thought was that Willie absolutely had to see this animal. I needed a witness to the beast, but on a more personal level, I wanted to share the amazing sight with Willie. This was something we would remember for life. The frog was grotesquely huge, and its size made it appear unusually primitive. Willie followed me straight to the prehistoric specimen, and we marveled from a safe distance. At first he didn't believe it was real. He found out I wasn't lying when he put his face as close as mine had been, and the frog blinked again. The blink had repulsed me and had made me draw away, but it had a different effect on Willie. Once he knew it was alive, he wanted to make it jump. I told him it was too big for that, but he assured me he knew exactly what to do. He ran away for a moment and returned with a curved, two-foot-long stick. He approached cautiously, and gently prodded the gargantuan critter. It didn't budge. Willie moved in again, crouched and ready for an instant retreat, and again gingerly poked the frog's bulging, blubbery gut area with the stick. This time it jumped. It uncoiled its nearly two-foot form into a slow-motion lunge and flew almost a full body-length before it landed, thudding horribly and jiggling on impact like a gelatinous blob of protoplasm. We were humored beyond description and, with our curiosity satisfied, we went back to our business and left the poor thing alone.

CHAPTER 20

THE LOG

Several more days passed. Willie and I continued to while away the time by playing cards, relaxing, and trying to restore our health. I was able to rein in the growing temptation to leave our hotel and explore our surroundings by reminding myself of the consequences of getting caught. That wasn't enough for Willie, though. He was far too restless to tolerate our self-imposed captivity for long. One day, just after the usual early-afternoon downpour, he announced that our hotel was near the edge of town, and that we were only a few minutes' walk to a trail he had seen leading out into the jungle. I couldn't understand how he knew so much about the area outside, but I guessed that he had been sneaking out and exploring while I was napping. He wanted to take a hike on the trail to see where it led. I told him he was crazy, but he wouldn't relent. He promised it would be safe and, even though I felt very uneasy, I agreed to go out and see what he was talking about.

We walked close to the buildings, listening intently for the army jeeps, but it was siesta hour and all was quiet. Sure enough, within three blocks of our hotel, he led me down a muddy road that soon narrowed into a foot trail that then disappeared into an overgrown field. Beyond the field was jungle.

"How did you find out about this place?" I asked as innocently as possible.

"I saw it that first night when we came here in the taxi," Willie shot back defensively. I suddenly felt the icy sting of betrayal and an edgy sort of vulnerability because I knew that was a blatant lie. My brother, perhaps my only true ally on the entire continent, was gambling with my safety and possibly my liberty, and there was nothing I could do about it. I weighed my options and, rather than risk a testy confrontation outside in a public place, I let the matter go. As we continued walking, I kept nervously looking back, expecting to see a jeep suddenly bear down on us, but we were alone. I felt better as we crossed the field, and I began to fully relax as we entered the jungle. There, we couldn't easily be seen and the sunlight dimmed as it filtered through dense foliage and the thirty-foot canopy. Within a quarter of a mile, our little trail was becoming completely overgrown, and soon we could not progress without ducking down and using both arms to clear the branches and vines.

I wondered who had carved out this path and where they had been trying to go. It was illogical that any trail would go a short distance and then simply end, but this one was disintegrating fast. I was about to suggest that if the way did not open up soon we should turn back, when I stepped over an unusual log. It lay square across the path and each end vanished into the bushes. I turned around in time to see Willie also step over the small, fallen tree trunk. There was something strange about it. Willie looked at me and then back down at the log. He had noticed it too. It was about six inches in diameter and a three-foot section of it was exposed on the pathway. I returned to it, and we squatted down to study the odd color pattern of the bark and the perfectly smooth, branch-free trunk. We both reached out and touched it at the same time, and our tree trunk suddenly undulated and slithered as only a snake can. It was instantly clear what we were dealing with, but neither of us knew whether the huge serpent's head was ahead of us or behind us on the trail. We whispered to each other that either retreating or advancing was a gamble and tried to make a decision. Given that we had just made it to that point unscathed, we hastily returned the way we had come without another word.

When we were at least a hundred feet away, we slowed our pace a bit and agreed it was best to return to our sanctuary. Only much later did we learn that that part of Bolivia is home to some of the largest anacondas on Earth.

CHAPTER 21

THE PUB

Almost every night, we walked down the street together to the mom-and-pop grocery store to stock up on supplies. By our second or third visit, we had become familiar with an elderly woman who attended the cash register. As our nightly trips to the *almacén* became routine, the woman began abandoning her post and disappearing into the back room as soon as we walked into the store. Moments later, a well developed but very young, scantily clad girl would emerge and take over the register. Willie and I took note of the not-so-subtle move and went about our shopping duties, always paying and leaving with a smile. We dubbed the young lady "Underwear Girl," in honor of what she was wearing every time we saw her. The older woman unfailingly played out the reverse bait-and-switch tactic every time we made an appearance. Willie explained to me that many poor families were convinced that their daughters would be much better off in life if they were to marry a "rich" American. One night, after the customary hustle played out, we walked out of the store marveling at the overt nature of it all. As we walked back to our hotel, we passed by all the usual stores and residences, and the one quiet bar that had been open every night, but which we had never been willing to enter.

Back in our room, we had barely unloaded our groceries when Willie became somewhat assertive.

"I think we should go back to that little tavern and have a drink," he declared. "It would do us some good to go in there, sit down, and have a beer." He went on and became more adamant. "Besides, we've earned it! And, by the way, I've been checking carefully every time we walk by and I have never seen a single military guy in that bar. I'm telling you, a time like this calls for a drink! Are you in?"

Willie was going to go with or without me and he had made a pretty good argument, so I acquiesced.

We set out on the short walk just in time to hear the roar of one of the jeeps as it sped around a corner six or eight blocks behind us and accelerated in our direction. My heart pounded as I scanned the storefronts for a place to hide, hoping we had not been seen. Willie was right with me, and we slithered into a narrow gap between two buildings and were out of sight as the jeep stormed by, bouncing almost out of control at the hands of its brash young driver. When the threat had passed and peace reigned again, we renewed our walk and were in the pub within a minute. We promptly found seats at an isolated small table with four chairs, and when asked by the bartender, we requested two beers.

As soon as our drinks had been served, an exuberant young man in his mid-twenties approached our table and asked if he could join us. We obliged, and he sat down and ordered a beer. He and Willie began talking, and Willie quickly explained that I didn't know Spanish and would not be able to participate in the conversation. But our new friend wanted to make me feel included, so he occasionally directed a simple phrase or two my way in broken English.

THE PUB

Willie solved our problem by becoming the translator. A quick, polite hand gesture from Willie every few minutes indicated to our drinking buddy that I needed to be filled in, and the strategy worked quite well. The young man asked where we were from and what on earth we were doing there.

"Wait…let me guess," he said before Willie could answer. "You're stuck here because of the train strike."

We laughed and gave him due credit for his correct, educated guess. Willie noted our friend's familiarity with train strikes and asked just how long, more or less, such train strikes tended to last.

"No problem," the guy answered. "They're almost always over within, say, five or six weeks."

Willie and I both strained to pretend that we, too, considered that a brief, completely acceptable period of time. A few swills later our friend noticed our beers were nearly empty and without asking, ordered another round. We warily went with the flow, smiling and thanking him but at the same time wondering what we might owe him for the small favor. Well into that round, we reciprocated, at which time he thanked us and said that would have to be his last one—he had to be at work bright and early the next day. The more we talked, the less concerned we became that the guy had any motives other than an honest, friendly chat with some travelers.

As the effects of the third beer began to sink in, he suddenly startled himself with his own brilliant idea. He apologized for the train strike and for how boring Puerto Suarez must seem to world travelers like us. He said he had a car and suggested that we tell him what hotel we were in. That way, after work tomorrow, he could swing by, pick us up, and show us what there was to see of the town. In fact, he offered to give us the grand tour.

"So how about it? Which hotel are you guys in?" he asked. "I'll meet you there tomorrow afternoon at four o'clock."

His cheeks were flushed and he was beaming from ear to ear. The offer was genuine. There was no ruse, and the ball was in our court. It was the moment of truth. Willie and I knew we had to say no, but we weren't sure what sort of an excuse to give. How could we turn down this act of kindness without offending the guy? He had thrown self-deprecating humor, generosity, and a genuine apology for his country's ineptitude on the line to be friendly. And now it was our turn. Even the slightest hesitation on our part could be misread and could prove deeply insulting. Willie and I exchanged very quick, subtle glances and Willie bought us a precious minute of deliberation by claiming he needed to translate for me. We readily agreed we would simply tell him the truth. If he reacted poorly, we would need to find another hotel and avoid the bar and the whole surrounding area for the rest of our time in town, and if he understood, we had nothing to fear. Willie carefully explained our predicament as our would-be tour guide attentively listened. He nodded often and seemed to get the picture. At one point in Willie's explanation, our host perked up markedly and began to chime in. There was a flurry of energetic verbal exchanges that ended with a lengthy contribution by our friend, and then Willie was doing all the nodding. Something so big had just happened that we all immediately needed another beer. Then it was time for Willie to translate the exchange to me.

It seemed our new friend was personally familiar with our nemesis out at the prison. We learned that our tormenter was the chief warden there, and that he had a reputation for being a sadist. He reportedly had a multitude of social shortcomings and made trouble wherever he went. Our friend had spent four years in the Bolivian Army stationed with this nasty, crude man and knew him well. He had even personally suffered a certain amount of bullying from him. He told us that there was an enormous, five-thousand-man military base—the largest in Bolivia—about twenty-five miles south of Puerto Suarez, out in the jungle. The prison, he said, was about three miles north of town. When the army had eventually become fed up with the wretched man, they relieved him of his duties at the base and put him in charge of the prison. The move was intended to put some distance between him and most of the other officers and recruits. Willie said our new friend was astounded, not that we had been rounded up and thrown into the prison, but that we had been let out. Apparently we were extremely lucky to have gotten out so soon and so unscathed. Our friend now completely understood why we did not want to go out and hang around in public places, and he agreed that we should hide out until the strike was over. He seemed to genuinely empathize with us and he sat there in silence for a few moments, pensively sipping his beer.

Just when it seemed there was nothing more to talk about, our buddy finished his last swig and hunched forward to offer one final tidbit of insider information. He said he had been out of the military for several years now, but recalled vividly that in years past, there had been several occasions when stranded train-strike victims had "hitched" a ride on the army's cargo plane during its weekly run back to Santa Cruz for supplies. The plane had routinely taken off every Tuesday morning at exactly seven o'clock. With just the right combination of timing, charm, personnel, and palm grease, we might have a chance to get a ride on that plane. We protested that going anywhere near a military installation would be a huge mistake but were assured that no one at the base liked the prison warden and that far out of town, we would be outside the sphere of his influence. The road to the base was unpaved and took two hours to traverse. We were advised to get up at four o'clock in the morning and take a taxi to the base. Next, we were to pay the driver some extra money to wait an hour in the event that we did not get the plane ride. Then all we needed was plenty of cash at the ready and a little luck. I was exhausted with nervous energy just listening to the plan. Our friend stood up, gave each of us a warm handshake, wished us all the best, and walked out of the bar. It was Thursday, and almost midnight.

The next days dragged by as we debated the plan and studied it from every angle. Willie thought it was worth a try, even given the risks of failure or capture. I was more inclined to go with the better-safe-than-sorry wait for the strike to be over. Ultimately, we would have to agree, because under no circumstances would each of us try something different. If we were nothing else, we were a team. In the end, Willie wore me down, and I reluctantly agreed to try to get a ride on the plane.

CHAPTER 22

THE DC-3

The annoying beep of the alarm clock pierced the early-morning darkness. It was three forty-five. Willie and I silently and methodically went about rising, packing, and slipping out of our hotel. We had paid our bill and were braced for whatever might come. We found a taxi at an intersection two blocks away and were soon well out of town and fully committed to our escape plan. Two hours later, at just past six o'clock, daylight had broken and our dreary pace slowed even more as we neared the huge military facility. The road abruptly widened and then its surface went from dirt to smooth pavement. Trees and brush gave way to large clearings, and there were now vehicles parked along both sides of the road. A hundred yards from the main gate, as if to keep his distance, our driver slowed, parked, and announced that this was it. We got out, paid him well for the ride and to wait an hour, and agreed on where he would be parked, should we need him. My heart raced. I felt removed from reality as I toughened up my stride, tried to appear confident and, side by side with Willie, approached the heavily guarded entrance gate.

When we were within talking distance of the nearest guard, he preemptively approached us and wanted to know what our business was. Willie explained that we would very much appreciate it if we could catch a ride on the plane that was going to Santa Cruz. The sentry laughed at us and explained that this was a military base, not an airport. Willie deftly slipped the man five U.S. dollars—about a week's pay in Bolivia at the time. The young man pocketed the money, hesitated for a second, and said to follow him. He said he would do his best to help us. He gestured to one of his fellow guards and the gate was opened. We entered the compound and heard the gate slam shut behind us. That particular clang stirred intense anxiety in me because it sounded just like the gate at the prison. We walked briskly, following our guide. A hundred yards into the trek, the three of us caught the attention of an officer whose uniform and stripes clearly advertised his superiority. As soon as he saw us, he walked over and intercepted us. He mildly admonished his underling, dismissed him, and stared us down like we were in deep trouble.

Again Willie calmly explained that we would be very grateful for the opportunity to ride aboard the plane that was going to Santa Cruz. Once more, we heard that this was a military facility, not a civilian airport, and that such things were not possible here. Then, just as before, Willie furtively slipped the man five dollars in U.S. currency. After thinking it over for a few seconds, the officer politely said to follow him, and that he would see what he could do to help us out. We walked another hundred yards, all the while heading directly toward an old DC-3 from the 1960s that sat idling on the tarmac. Within two minutes, just like clockwork, an even higher-ranking officer moved in and confronted us. He briefly scolded and then dismissed his subordinate, sending him back to his previous post. He looked us up and down the way a party host might eye an uninvited and very unwelcome guest. This man had so many medals he jingled when he walked. He obviously was at or very near the top of the military food chain. He was not accustomed to being manipulated or taking orders—he was used to giving them. We must have looked pathetic because he interrogated us as if we were having a conversation rather than as if we had done something wrong. We were totally at his mercy and all three of us knew it.

Willie humbly explained that the train strike had rendered us in need of a ride to Santa Cruz, but that we did not expect something for nothing. He made it clear that we would be happy to pay any necessary fees. The plane was now so close that conversation was difficult without raised voices. Willie reiterated that we were not freeloaders and would gladly pay our fare in full. The man reflected for a moment and then leaned close to Willie's face. He said a ride could be arranged for fifty U.S. dollars each. Cash. Right here, right now. To us, that was a deal. Willie told me to get out my money. He grabbed my stash, combined it with his own, counted out one hundred dollars, and paid the man. The officer looked it over for a second, counted it, and put it in his front pants pocket. Then he said to follow him, and he turned and began walking toward the plane.

At the foot of the portable rollaway stairs that led up to the plane's door, the officer stopped, and with an upward-sweeping gesture of his left arm, indicated that we should ascend. We nodded obligingly and started up the steps. Halfway to the top, Willie saved our hides again. He paused and gained the officer's attention just as he was turning to walk away. Willie politely asked if the man could please explain to the others on the plane that we had paid, so they would realize that we were official. Our well-paid partner-in-crime smiled knowingly, strode smartly toward the narrow staircase and marched swiftly to the top, squeezing past both of us on the way up. He passed through the open door and entered the fuselage. We were right behind him and noticed that everyone on board immediately stopped what they were doing and saluted him resolutely. When the dozen soldiers on the plane were all at attention, the big cheese announced to them that these two *gringos* had paid. We were to be given a seat, flown back to

Santa Cruz, escorted to the exit of the base, and left alone. Anyone who did not adhere to his instructions would answer to him personally. He then reassured us that everything was in order and walked out the door, down the stairs, and was gone.

Willie and I were each quickly assigned to a low-slung, canvas, parachute-jumper type of seat, which faced perpendicular to the direction of travel and swung from an overhead bar. The whole scene was very odd, so we just shut up and sat down as we were told. We had been on the plane less than fifteen minutes when the door was slammed shut. In another minute the motors revved up, the plane shook, shuddered, and started to move, and we took off.

Once we were in the air, I couldn't help but consider that the soldiers could do anything they wanted to us. Horrifying memories flooded over me of film footage I had seen of soldiers throwing captured enemies out of helicopter doors during the Vietnam War. But I needed to appear—and above all, remain—calm. Our fate was totally in their hands and everyone on the plane was aware of the imbalance of power. Clearly, they realized that they could throw us out to our deaths if they felt like it, and that no one would ever even find our bodies. But was that their plan? I was afraid to even look at any of them, especially straight in the eyes. I curled up and kept to myself for nearly an hour before I relaxed a little and surveyed the plane's interior in more detail. A soldier directly across from me noticed my curiosity and gave me an acknowledging, friendly little nod. For the first time in many days, perhaps even weeks, I felt like everything was going to be okay. My spirits were elevated so quickly that I even dared at one point to leave my seat, clamber over to one of the little windows, and look out. Below me lay the vast jungle for as far as the eye could see. And there in the foreground, crystal clear before me, were the dreaded railroad tracks whose every inch had tormented us going the other way.

We soon landed and were escorted off the plane and to the exit of the base by a couple of very businesslike young soldiers who were not in the mood to chat. And that was that. Suddenly the enormity of the ordeal registered with me and probably with Willie, too. I wasn't even sure how I was supposed to feel. We had been relentlessly attacked and bitten by mosquitos, derailed, abandoned, starved, imprisoned, and emotionally tortured. And now, we were back in the "normal" world, exactly where we had started from more than two weeks earlier, as if nothing had ever happened.

Ultimately, we had not accomplished a single one of our objectives, but what mattered most was that we were safe. It was time to cut our losses and move forward. We were due in Cochabamba at some point soon, but we had totally lost track of time. I asked Willie when we were supposed to start our Spanish lessons, but we couldn't agree on how many days we had been gone. I had started the trip with a watch that showed the time, day of the week, and calendar date, but it had mysteriously quit working on the second day in Puerto Suarez. Willie didn't like wristwatches and had never worn one. We caught the next available flight to Cochabamba and found Blanca waiting for us. She never specifically said so, but I think we were a couple of days late for our lessons.

CHAPTER 23

THE FEVER

We knew we were in town for the long haul, so we started off in a basic hostel near the town square but began to look for more permanent lodging. Through an ad in the local newspaper, we found a room on the second floor of a family's house. The room would accommodate both of us and cost about sixty dollars a month. The rent included meals, kitchen and living room privileges, and laundry service. So we went there, talked with the people, and agreed to pay for two months up front.

Things weren't perfect, but went well enough with a few modifications on our part. The first few meals with the family caused us some rather debilitating intestinal consternation, so we resorted to buying and preparing our own food. The beds in our room sagged miserably in the middle because of the poorly designed frame and the weak support springs, so we disassembled them, stored the hardware in the closet, and simply placed the mattresses on the floor. That arrangement was infinitely more comfortable. We were within walking distance of Blanca's house and as we got to know the family and the other people in our neighborhood, it appeared we would settle into a nice routine. I could finally sink my teeth into learning Spanish, which had been my original goal.

On the third day of classes, I left my lesson for the usual walk home but was soon overcome with a profound fatigue, as if I had been drugged. I started to perspire profusely, my vision blurred, and I was so weak I could hardly make it home. The onslaught was very sudden and very potent. I dragged myself up the stairs and collapsed onto my mattress. I mentioned to Willie that I felt terrible and asked if he would please get me some water. All water intended for drinking needed to be boiled at least twenty minutes to kill the germs, so Willie went to the kitchen, grabbed the nearest pot, and boiled me up some water. The pot had just been used to cook rice and Willie had not bothered to clean it, but as things turned out, the little bits of rice may have been a good thing.

I then lost the next five weeks of my life. Almost the only memories I have are of focusing all my energy to get my head to roll from one side to the other so the pillow would feel cool. I have vague, dreamlike memories of asking Willie for more water and him always bringing me the same pot with little pieces of rice in it. I also remember him coming in one day and telling me that I looked like death warmed over and that if I didn't look better in a few days, he was going to carry me to the airport, put me on a plane, and send me home. He said that if I died there in Bolivia, everyone at home would be mad at him for not doing enough to help me. One day he reported that he had gone to a Swiss pharmacy and precisely described my symptoms to them. He said they had given him some little pills for me and that I should take them. He claimed that in Bolivia, a good pharmacist knew better than the average doctor how to solve medical problems like mine, including which pills to give for each respective ailment. So I took the pills as directed, thinking I didn't have much to lose, and in a few days I actually began to feel better. Soon I was occasionally lucid and realized that I could, at any time, fly home to the United States and recover from whatever was wrong with me. But in truth, I wanted to stay.

I continued to drift into and out of reality for another week, but I spent more time awake and alert with each passing day. More than a month into the illness, things were finally looking up. Soon, I could sit up a little to drink my water with the rice grains in it, and one day I finally felt like I needed to use the bathroom. I'm sure it wasn't the first time in a month that I had to use a toilet, and that Willie had been helping me with those needs, but I just couldn't remember any of it. I hobbled into the bathroom, holding onto the walls for support along the way, and startled myself when I looked into the mirror. I saw, looking back at me, as close to that hollow-cheeked, starving-person image as I had ever seen in real life. I knew the look mainly from films of the liberation at the end of the Holocaust. It was shocking. I had lost at least twenty-five pounds—and I had been thin to begin with. I consoled myself by thinking only of how much better I was feeling lately, and how much more mentally astute I was becoming day by day. Within the next forty-eight hours it was obvious that the Swiss pharmacist had called it right.

CHAPTER 24

THE OMELET

I was well on the way to recovery, and for the first time in ages, I actually felt hungry. Willie was very happy and wanted to celebrate by cooking me a gigantic meal of my choice. So I told him I wanted an omelet, a cheese omelet. He declared that he was an absolute expert at preparing that particular delicacy and offered to go to the market, buy all the necessary ingredients, and cook me up a superlative example. As he descended the stairs and we loudly exchanged a verbal list of what he would need from the market, the father of the household overheard us and asked what was going on. Willie filled him in on the details and the dad announced that he, too, was an expert at making omelets. He suggested that he and Willie go to the market together and that he would make omelets for his family for dinner as well. In fact, if I could make it downstairs, he said, we would all eat and celebrate together. About an hour later there was great noise and energy as Willie and the señor returned. It sounded a lot like they had stopped for a drink or two on the way home from the market.

Soon the smell of grilled onions, peppers, mushrooms, tomatoes, fried eggs, and melted cheese filled the room. The man of the house and Willie had taken over the kitchen, warning all the females to steer clear, and were cooking up a storm. I cautiously descended the staircase with wobbly knees and found them in the kitchen in a very competitive and animated state. They were slicing and dicing and loudly describing everything related to the proper making of an omelet. They also seemed to have elevated the whole thing to a macho contest of some sort. I took a seat at the table, across the room from the impromptu cook-off. Among the others assembled, I was selected to be a judge of whose omelet was the best, and I looked forward to it. In no time, Willie was serving me a beautiful, world-class specimen. Within a few seconds I figured out what Willie and the señor had been so competitively arguing about, namely, who could tolerate the hottest chili peppers.

To my horror, Willie had arranged it so that the first mouthful of solid food I ate after the longest period of fasting in my life, was a burning hot, utterly inedible chili-pepper assault. In a couple of seconds, I went from normal and hungry to very miserable and totally unable to chew or swallow. I could barely even breathe. My throat, lips, and tongue were in terrible pain. I got up from the table, staggered around as tears streamed from my eyes, and tried to find some water. One could not simply drink from the faucet, so I needed to find a stash of cool, pre-boiled water, but did not know where to find one. I communicated my problem as best I could but was not taken very seriously by anyone, and I ended up recovering on my own over the next several hours. Willie and the father couldn't figure out why I was such a lightweight. They made their own omelets even stronger and ate them, and mine too. They called it a tie and agreed to celebrate by going out for a few beers. I gave Willie as stern an admonition as I could muster, but he seemed unfazed and still thought the omelet was fine and that I was just a wimp.

CHAPTER 25

LA PAZ

As the next few days went by, I rapidly grew healthier and came to realize just how sick I had been and for how long. With a little coaxing, I was able to get Willie to tell me exactly what pills I had been taking and what diagnosis the pharmacist had made based on my symptoms. It was typhoid fever. I traced its likely origins back to the water I had drunk from the burbling little spring at the muddy puddle in the jungle.

I also discovered that we had lost our time slot with Blanca, because while I was ill, Willie had stopped going to the lessons, too. I decided that when I was eventually strong enough to walk comfortably again, I wanted to leave Cochabamba. Willie suggested we briefly visit the national capital, La Paz, and then leave Bolivia altogether and trek north to Peru to breathe some new life into our trip.

When my appetite for everything except chili peppers had returned to normal and I was ambulatory again without much help, Willie and I boarded a train for La Paz. We experienced only one minor, eight-hour delay underway—the result of a bad clutch—and had an otherwise fascinating ride up onto the cool, wind-swept Bolivian high plains in the eastern shadow of the Andes. When we arrived at the highest-elevation capital city in the world, we transferred to a bus and rode down into the bowl-shaped city of La Paz. As I took in our new surroundings, it was clear to me that phase one of the trip was over.

We had been through some very difficult times during the first two months. My relationship with Willie had been tested, my health and safety had been seriously threatened, and adapting to the culture had not been easy. As for picking up the language, I was way behind schedule, but I still had every intention of learning Spanish. In spite of the challenges, the trip thus far had been educational, memorable, and full of adventure. After several days in La Paz, Willie and

I boarded a bus and left Bolivia. I felt optimistic and energized as I looked forward to what was ahead in Peru.

About the Author

F.P. Nieman is a foreign-language teacher who has worked at Independence High School in San Jose, California, for more than thirty years. He was trained and worked as an auto mechanic, but eventually he answered an inner calling to see the world and study languages, which led to his teaching career.

He has traveled through much of the United States, Canada, Mexico, the Caribbean, South America, Europe, and Asia. Raised in a family of ten, he had moved eight times before he was fourteen years old. Nieman's extensive travels inspired him to write the nonfiction books, *Under Every Stone* and *The Sunbaked Tin Can*.

He holds a BA in German from the University of California, Berkeley, a teaching credential from California State University, Hayward, and an MA in education from San Jose State University. He currently lives in San Ramon, California, and enjoys summers in Anacortes, Washington.

Made in the USA
San Bernardino, CA
02 September 2015